EFFICIENT AND ACCURATE PARALLEL GENETIC ALGORITHMS

GENETIC ALGORITHMS AND EVOLUTIONARY COMPUTATION

EFFICIENT AND ACCURATE PARALLEL GENETIC ALGORITHMS

by

Erick Cantú-Paz
Lawrence Livermore National Lab, U.S.A.

KLUWER ACADEMIC PUBLISHERS
Boston / Dordrecht / London

Distributors for North, Central and South America:
Kluwer Academic Publishers
101 Philip Drive
Assinippi Park
Norwell, Massachusetts 02061 USA
Telephone (781) 871-6600
Fax (781) 871-6528
E-Mail <kluwer@wkap.com>

Distributors for all other countries:
Kluwer Academic Publishers Group
Distribution Centre
Post Office Box 322
3300 AH Dordrecht, THE NETHERLANDS
Telephone 31 78 6392 392
Fax 31 78 6546 474
E-Mail <services@wkap.nl>

 Electronic Services <http://www.wkap.nl>

Library of Congress Cataloging-in-Publication Data

A C.I.P. Catalogue record for this book is available
from the Library of Congress.

Printed on acid-free paper.

Printed in the United States of America

The Publisher offers discounts on this book for course use and bulk purchases.
For further information, send email to <lance.wobus@wkap.com>

To Javiera and our baby

Series Foreword
Genetic Algorithms and Evolutionary Computation

David E. Goldberg, Consulting Editor
University of Illinois at Urbana-Champaign
Email: deg@uiuc.edu

Researchers and practitioners alike are increasingly turning to search, optimization, and machine-learning procedures based on natural selection and natural genetics to solve problems across the spectrum of human endeavor. These *genetic algorithms* and techniques of *evolutionary computation* are solving problems and inventing new hardware and software that rival human designs. *Genetic Algorithms and Evolutionary Computation* publishes research monographs, edited collections, and graduate-level texts in this rapidly growing field. Primary areas of coverage include the theory, implementation, and application of genetic algorithms (GAs), evolution strategies (ESs), evolutionary programming (EP), learning classifier systems (LCSs) and other variants of genetic and evolutionary computation (GEC). The series also publishes texts in related fields such as artificial life, adaptive behavior, artificial immune systems, agent-based systems, neural computing, fuzzy systems, and quantum computing as long as GEC techniques are part of or inspiration for the system being described.

Erick Cantú-Paz's monograph is the first book in this series, and in many ways it is an exemplar of the kind of book we hope to attract. The book is an elaboration of Erick's groundbreaking dissertation on the design of efficient parallel genetic algorithms. It combines *facetwise* and exact design theory, careful bounding empirical investigation, and a keen eye toward practice in a text that has been written in an accessible, logical, and thorough manner. In the end, it gives us critical scaling laws that accurately govern the particular parallel architectures that have been analyzed and that approximately bound many architectures that have not. I believe it is fair to say that prior to this work, the design of parallel GAs was something of an empirical black art, guided largely by ad hoc trial and error experimentation. Following this work, the solution quality, duration, connectivity, deme size, deme count, and migration rates succumb to the magic of Erick's careful analysis, experimentation, and exposition. This is not to say that parallel GAs are now completely understood. The very nature of complex systems design almost ensures that we can never get to the bottom of the subject. On the other hand, our understanding of parallel GAs is much enhanced by this work, and I urgently recommend that all readers interested in parallel genetic and evolutionary algorithms study this important book carefully and soon.

Contents

Preface

As genetic algorithms (GAs) become increasingly popular, they are applied to difficult problems that may require considerable computations. In such cases, parallel implementations of GAs become necessary to reach high-quality solutions in reasonable times. But, even though their mechanics are simple, parallel GAs are complex non-linear algorithms that are controlled by many parameters, which are not well understood.

This book is about the design of parallel GAs. It presents theoretical developments that improve our understanding of the effect of the algorithm's parameters on its search for quality and efficiency. These developments are used to formulate guidelines on how to choose the parameter values that minimize the execution time while consistently reaching solutions of high quality.

The book can be read in several ways, depending on the readers' interests and their previous knowledge about these algorithms. Newcomers to the field will find the background material in each chapter useful to become acquainted with previous work, and to understand the problems that must be faced to design efficient and reliable algorithms. Potential users of parallel GAs that may have doubts about their practicality or reliability may be more confident after reading this book and understanding the algorithms better. Those who are ready to try a parallel GA on their applications may choose to skim through the background material, and use the results directly without following the derivations in detail. These readers will find that using the results can help them to choose the type of parallel GA that best suits their needs, without having to invest the time to implement and test various options. Once that is settled, even the most experienced users dread the long and frustrating experience of configuring their algorithms by trial and error. The guidelines contained herein will shorten dramatically the time spent tweaking the algorithm, although some experimentation may still be needed for fine-tuning.

In addition to the results that practitioners will find applicable to the design of parallel GAs, those interested in the mathematical analysis of GAs may find the techniques used here useful for their own endeavors. Indeed, some of the analysis presented here is relevant not only to parallel GAs, but also to their serial counterparts.

This book is based on my Ph.D. dissertation (Cantu-Paz, 1999a) The presentation of the material assumes that the reader has a good understanding of the basic concepts of GAs and statistics. However, some of the derivations use concepts that may not be familiar to many readers, and so I explain them briefly the first time that they appear.

Organization

The first chapter contains a brief introduction to GAs. In addition, it presents the four common types of parallel GAs, and it explains the design problems that users face when using these algorithms.

Chapters 2 and 3 are about GAs with a single population. Chapter 2 deals with finding an appropriate population size for simple serial GAs, and introduces an abstract model of GAs that will be used in the remainder of the book to study parallel GAs. Chapter 3 shows how to parallelize GAs using a simple master-slave algorithm, and how to minimize its execution time. Since this is the simplest parallel algorithm that we examine, we consider this case to be the lower bound on the acceptable performance of parallel GAs. Other parallel GAs should perform better than the simple master-slave.

Most of the book focuses on algorithms with multiple populations. These are the most popular parallel GAs and potentially the most efficient, because they require fewer communications than the master-slave. Unfortunately, they are also the most complex, as one must face difficult and interrelated design alternatives. Some of the main problems are to determine (1) the size and the number of demes (subpopulations), (2) the topology that interconnects the demes, and (3) the migration rate that controls how many individuals migrate between demes.

It is difficult to study all these problems at once, so we consider first two cases that represent lower and upper bounds of the migration rate and the connectivity between demes. Practitioners do not use these extreme cases very often, but the analysis sheds some light on the intermediate configurations, and introduces the methodology that will be used in the following chapters.

The study of bounding cases spans two chapters. First, Chapter 4 extends the population sizing theory of serial GAs to the parallel bounding cases, and shows how to minimize the execution time while maintaining a constant target solution quality. Then, Chapter 5 uses Markov chains to analyze the long-term behavior of communicating demes.

Chapter 5 also introduces the first model for intermediate topologies. This initial model is very accurate, but it requires considerable computations, and may not be practical to study large numbers of demes. Nevertheless, the Markov chains are used to verify the accuracy of the simpler models derived in the next chapter. Chapter 6 finds approximate equations that capture the effects of the topology and migration rate on the quality and cost of multi-deme GAs. These simple models are then used to minimize the execution time.

Chapter 7 studies how the individuals that migrate between populations may affect the speed of convergence of the algorithm. The controversial issue of superlinear speedups in parallel GAs is explored in detail in this chapter.

At this point, the book has investigated the benefits of master-slave and multiple-deme parallel GAs in isolation, but they may be combined into hierarchical algorithms that offer even greater advantages. Chapter 8 describes how to minimize the execution time by allocating the available processors to combinations of demes and slaves. This chapter also includes a discussion on fine-grained parallel GAs, and it contains a complete step-by-step example that illustrates how to determine the optimal configuration of a parallel GA for a particular problem and hardware environment.

Finally, Chapter 9 contains a summary of the results, recommendations for further research, and the conclusions of this study.

Acknowledgments

Undoubtedly, the person who most influenced this work is my Ph.D. advisor, David E. Goldberg. I wish to thank him for his guidance, support, and encouragement during my time at the University of Illinois. Besides of many technical and methodological issues, I learned from him much about the "human side" of engineering.

I wish to thank Prof. Geneva Belford, Prof. Sylvian Ray, and Prof. Josep Torrellas for their comments on my work and for their patience when delays occurred. During my stay at Illinois, I had the opportunity to learn many different things as I worked with each of them.

I was very fortunate to be surrounded by a very productive and cheerful research group in the Illinois Genetic Algorithms Lab. There are very few places in the world where one has access to so many resources to do research on genetic algorithms and have so much fun at the same time. I wish to thank all the students, visitors, and librarians at IlliGAL for their friendship and for all the technical discussions.

Numerous anonymous reviewers made useful comments on parts of this book that have been submitted to conferences and journals. I am grateful for their careful reading of the papers, and for their suggestions that helped to improve the exposition of some of the ideas contained here.

My explorations of parallel GAs began when I was an undergraduate student at the Instituto Tecnológico Autónomo de México. Back then, my advisor, Marcelo Mejía, encouraged me to work on a senior project on parallel GAs, a topic about which neither of us knew much. I was lucky to have the support of Marcelo and the help of other professors such as Francisco Cervantes, José Incera, and Carlos Zozaya, who also served as a model and inspiration. That experience with the senior project taught me about the fun of research, which continued in graduate school and beyond.

My sisters and I were blessed with wonderful parents who gave us the perfect example of how to live a happy life. No words can express my gratitude for everything that they have done; I can only hope to be able to transmit their wisdom to my own children.

Finally, I thank Javiera, my wife, for all her love and understanding, both in graduate school and during the preparation of this book. Her support kept me going during hard and sometimes frustrating times.

My research was sponsored by a number of sources: a Fulbright-García Robles Fellowship, administered by USIA and by CONACyT; a teaching assistantship from the Department of Computer Science, UIUC; and a research assistantship from the Beckman Institute, UIUC. The work was sponsored by the Air Force Office of Scientific Research, Air Force Materiel Command, USAF, under grants number F49620-94-1-0103, F49620-95-1-0338 and F49620-97-1-0050. Research funding for this project was also provided by a grant from the US Army Research Laboratory Program, Cooperative Agreement DAAL01-96-2-003. The US Government is authorized to reproduce and distribute reprints for governmental purposes notwithstanding any copyright notation thereon. The views and conclusions contained herein are those of the authors and should not be interpreted as necessarily representing the official policies and endorsements, either expressed or implied, of the Air Force Office of Scientific Research or the US Government.

Portions of this work were performed under the auspices of the U.S. Department of Energy by University of California Lawrence Livermore National Laboratory under contract No. W-7405-Eng-48.

Chapter 1

INTRODUCTION

Genetic Algorithms (GAs) are search methods based on principles of natural selection and genetics. They have been applied successfully to numerous problems in business, engineering, and science (Goldberg, 1994). In many practical applications, GAs find good solutions in reasonable amounts of time. However, in some cases, GAs may require hundreds of thousands of expensive function evaluations, and depending on the cost of each evaluation, the GA may take days, months, or even years to find an acceptable solution.

There have been multiple efforts to make GAs faster, and one of the most promising alternatives is to use parallel implementations. The parallel nature of genetic algorithms has been recognized for a long time, and many have successfully used parallel GAs to reduce the time required to reach acceptable solutions to complex problems. GAs work with a population of independent solutions, which makes it easy to distribute the computational load among several processors. Indeed, GAs are "embarrassingly parallel" in the sense that it is very easy to implement them efficiently on parallel computers. However, despite of their operational simplicity, parallel GAs are complex non-linear algorithms that are controlled by many parameters that affect their efficiency and the quality of their search. Setting those parameters correctly is crucial to obtain good solutions quickly and reliably.

In particular, the design of parallel GAs involves choices such as using a single or multiple populations. In either case, the size of the populations must be determined carefully, and for multiple populations, one must decide how many to use. In addition, the populations may remain isolated or they may communicate by exchanging individuals or some other information. Communication involves extra costs and additional decisions on the pattern of communications, on the number of individuals to be exchanged, and on the frequency of communications.

Typically, the parameters of parallel GAs are found by systematic experimentation or just by chance. These approaches often result in a waste of computing resources or in an inadequate search quality, and practitioners may dismiss parallel GAs as being impractical or unreliable.

The goal of this book is to go beyond this ad-hoc tuning of parameters, and provide guidelines to choose their values rationally. The result are efficient parallel GAs that consistently reach solutions of high quality.

The research described here combines theory and experiments to develop equations that capture the effect of the parameters on the speed and quality of the algorithm. This study does not develop exact models of every facet of (parallel) genetic algorithms, because exact and complete models would probably be too difficult and expensive to use, and therefore would have little practical significance. Instead, the intention of this book is to present simple approximate models that are easy to calibrate to the particular problem and to the hardware used in the implementation.

Certainly, in the short term, faster implementations that result only from hardware improvements will be sufficient to solve many current problems satisfactorily; but, in the long run, the increasing complexity of the problems will supersede any hardware advancements. Since the models introduced in this book can be calibrated to consider future developments in hardware, we will be able to design algorithms that exploit those developments, without having to experiment blindly with all possible settings of the parameters.

The next section gives a very brief introduction to simple genetic algorithms. It defines some terms that will be used in the remainder of the book, and it describes how a simple GA works, but it is not a complete tutorial on GAs. Interested readers may consult the book by Goldberg (1989a) for more detailed background information on GAs. Section 2 describes the different types of parallel GAs that will be examined in the book. Section 3 ends the chapter with a brief summary.

1   AN INTRODUCTION TO GENETIC ALGORITHMS

Genetic algorithms are stochastic search algorithms based on principles of natural selection and genetics. GAs attempt to find good solutions to the problem at hand by manipulating a population of candidate solutions.

Each member of the population is typically represented by a single chromosome, which can be as simple as a string of zeroes and ones, or as complex as a computer program. The chromosome encodes a solution to the problem. The initial population is generated randomly, unless some good solutions are known, or there is a heuristic to generate good solutions to the problem. In the latter case, a portion of the population is still generated randomly to ensure that there is some diversity in the population.

The individuals are evaluated to determine how well they solve the problem with a fitness function, which is unique to each problem, and must be supplied by the user of the algorithm. In particular, GAs are often used as optimizers, and the fitness of an individual is typically the value of the objective function at the point represented by the chromosome. The individuals with better performance are selected as parents of the next generation. GAs create new individuals using simple randomized operators that resemble sexual recombination (crossover) and mutation in natural organisms. The new solutions are evaluated with the fitness function, and the cycle of selection, recombination, and mutation is repeated until a user-defined termination criterion is satisfied.

GAs are controlled by several inputs, such as the size of the population, and the rates that control how often mutation and crossover are used. GAs are not guaranteed to converge to the optimal solution, but a careful manipulation of the input parameters and choosing a representation that is adequate to the problem increase the chances of success.

The size of the population is important because it influences whether the GA can find good solutions and the time that it takes to reach them (Goldberg et al., 1992; Harik et al., 1997). If the population is too small, the solution space may not be sampled properly, and it will be difficult to identify good solutions. If the population is too big, the GA will waste computational resources processing unnecessary individuals. The question of how to determine the size of the population of a simple GA will be examined in detail in Chapter 2, and will be a central question in our investigation of parallel GAs.

There are many ways to encode a solution in the chromosomes, and there are many variations of selection, crossover, and mutation. Some of these variations are better suited to a particular problem than others, and it has been proven that no single choice is the best for all problems (Wolpert & Macready, 1997).

As was mentioned above, the simplest encodings use chromosomes composed of zeroes and ones, but other encodings may be more natural to the problem and may facilitate the search for good solutions. The choice of encodings is related to the operators that produce new individuals from the selected ones. Mutation is the simplest operator, and it acts by altering some random value within a chromosome. For example, take a binary chromosome $A = 1\ 1\ 0\ 1\ 1$ and assume that position 3 is chosen randomly to mutate. The new chromosome would be $A' = 1\ 1\ 1\ 1\ 1$. As in nature, in GAs the probability of applying mutation is very low. Crossover is considered the primary exploration operator in GAs. In its simplest form, this operator chooses randomly two individuals from those previously selected and exchanges substrings around a single randomly-chosen crossover point. As an example, consider strings A_1 and A_2 of length $l = 8$:

$$A_1 = 0\ 1\ 1\ 0\ |\ 1\ 1\ 1\ 1$$
$$A_2 = 1\ 1\ 1\ 0\ |\ 0\ 0\ 0\ 0$$

The crossover point is indicated by the symbol $|$. Exchanging substrings around the crossover point results in two new individuals for the next generation:

$$A_1' = 0\ 1\ 1\ 0\ 0\ 0\ 0\ 0$$
$$A_2' = 1\ 1\ 1\ 0\ 1\ 1\ 1\ 1$$

This example used 1-point crossover, but it is possible to use 2-point, n-point, or uniform crossover. Uniform crossover consists on choosing each bit of the offspring randomly from each of the parents. More crossover points result in a more exploratory search, but also increase the chance of destroying good solutions. There are interesting variants of crossover that wonder away from the biological metaphor and combine material from more than than two parents to produce offspring (Eiben, Raué, & Ruttkay, 1994; Eiben & Bäck, 1997).

There are also many alternatives to select the parents. Each selection method has different characteristics, but they all share the same objective of preserving the good individuals and discarding the less fit. One popular selection method is tournament selection. It consists on obtaining a small random sample of individuals from the population and choosing the best one of the sample to survive. This is repeated as necessary to select as many parents as needed for the next generation. We will revisit selection in more detail in Chapter 7, but all of the experiments in the intermediate chapters use tournament selection.

There are several ways to stop a GA. One simple method is to stop after a predetermined number of generations or function evaluations. Another method is to stop when the average quality of the population does not improve after some number of generations. In addition, the algorithm can terminate when all the individuals are identical, which can only occur if no mutation is used.

The basic mechanism in GAs is Darwinian evolution: bad traits are eliminated from the population because they appear in individuals which do not survive the process of selection. The good traits survive and are mixed by recombination (crossover) to form new—and possible better—individuals. The notion of "good" traits can be formalized with the concept of building blocks (BBs), which are templates (schemata) that match a short well-adapted set of features that are common to good solutions. The next section will explain BBs and schemata in more detail and more formally.

1.1   SCHEMATA, PARTITIONS, AND BUILDING BLOCKS

Although most GA practitioners are familiar with the concepts of partitions, schemata, and building blocks, some of the models presented in this book are based on these concepts, and thus a brief description may be useful to avoid misunderstandings.

As we saw in the previous section, it is common practice to encode the variables of the problem at hand as binary strings. Of course, alphabets of higher cardinalities may be used, but without loss of generality we restrict the discussion to binary alphabets. Borrowing some terminology from Biology, in the binary case we say that there are two possible alleles (0 and 1) for each locus (position in the chromosome).

A *schema* is a string over the extended alphabet $\{0, 1, *\}$, and it represents the set of individuals that have 0 or 1 in exactly the same positions as the schema. The $*$ is a "don't care" symbol that matches anything. For example, in a domain that uses 8-bit long strings, the set of individuals that start with 1 and have a 0 in the second position are represented by the schema $10 * * * * * *$.

The number k of fixed positions in a schema is its order. Recognizing that each of the k fixed positions can be 0 or 1, a particular schema of order k denotes one of 2^k possible classes in the search space. Continuing with the example from above, $10 * * * * * *$ is one of the $2^2 = 4$ mutually-exclusive sets of individuals that can be specified by fixing the first and second positions of a schemata. The other sets in the same partition are $00 * * * * * *$, $01 * * * * * *$, and $11 * * * * * *$.

We can represent a *partition* of the search space using a template where the k fixed positions of the schemata in the partition are represented by a metasymbol F. In our example, the space is partitioned into mutually-exclusive sets by the four schemata with fixed symbols in their first two positions: $FF * * * * * * *$.

Not all the schemata in a partition are equal. Some schemata represent classes of individuals with a higher average fitness than others, and some schemata actually match portions of the global solution. Note that it is possible that some schemata have a high average fitness, but do not match the global optimum. In fact, test functions that deceive the

GA to converge to suboptimal schemata in a partition have been proposed (Goldberg, 1987; Goldberg, 1992; Deb & Goldberg, 1994), and are used in several studies—including this one—to test theoretical models of convergence quality.

Low-order highly-fit schemata are sometimes called *building blocks* (BBs) (Goldberg, 1989a). In this book, we refer to the lowest-order schema that consistently leads to the global optimum as the correct BB. In this view, the correct BB must (1) match the global optimum *and* (2) have the highest average fitness of all the schemata in the same partition. All other schemata in the partition are labeled as incorrect. Also in this view, the juxtaposition of two BBs of order k at a particular string does not lead to a BB of order $2k$, but instead to two separate BBs (the papers by Goldberg et al. (1992) and Thierens and Goldberg (1993) are early examples of this view).

It is important to note that genetic algorithms do not manipulate schemata or building blocks explicitly. Schemata are abstract devices that we can use to construct models that predict how GAs work, and that can be used to design more efficient and accurate algorithms.

2   A CLASSIFICATION OF PARALLEL GAs

The basic idea behind most parallel programs is to divide a large problem into smaller tasks and to solve the tasks simultaneously using multiple processors. This divide-and-conquer approach can be applied to GAs in many different ways, and the literature contains numerous examples of successful parallel implementations. Some parallelization methods use a single population, while others divide the population into several relatively isolated subpopulations. Some methods exploit massively parallel computer architectures, while others are better suited to multicomputers with fewer and more powerful processing elements connected by a slower network.

The classification of parallel GAs used in this book is similar to others used in literature reviews (Adamidis, 1994; Lin et al., 1994; Alba & Troya, 1999; Tomassini, 1999). We can recognize four major types of parallel GAs:

1. Single-population master-slave GAs,

2. Multiple-population GAs,

3. Fine-grained GAs,

4. Hierarchical hybrids

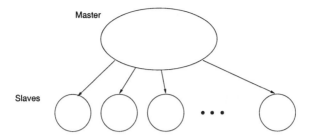

Figure 1.1. A schematic of a master-slave parallel GA. The master stores the population, executes the GA operations, and distributes individuals to the slaves. The slaves evaluate the fitness of the individuals.

Master-slave GAs have a single population. One master node executes the GA (selection, crossover, and mutation), and the evaluation of fitness is distributed among several slave processors (see Figure 1.1). The slaves evaluate the fitness of the individuals that they receive from the master and return the results. Since in this type of parallel GAs selection and crossover consider the entire population, master-slave GAs are also known as "global" parallel GAs. These algorithms are the topic of Chapter 3.

Multiple-population or multiple-deme GAs are more sophisticated.[1] They consist on several subpopulations that exchange individuals occasionally (Figure 1.2 has a schematic). This exchange of individuals is called migration, and it is controlled by several parameters. Multiple-deme GAs are very popular, but they are the class of parallel GAs that is most difficult to control, because the effects of migration are not understood very well. In particular, users of these algorithms have to determine the number and size of the demes, the frequency of migration, the number and destination of migrants, and the method used to select which individuals migrate. These are complex questions that occupy most of the book: this class of parallel GAs will be examined in Chapters 4 to 7.

Multiple-deme parallel GAs are known with different names. Sometimes they are known as "distributed" GAs, because they are usually implemented on distributed-memory MIMD computers. Since the computation to communication ratio is usually high, they are occasionally called "coarse-grained GAs". Also, multiple-deme GAs resemble the "island model" of population genetics that considers a population split

---

[1]We use the terms deme or subpopulation to refer to a set of individuals that compete and breed among themselves: a simple GA has only one deme, and each of the subpopulations of a island model GA is a separate deme.

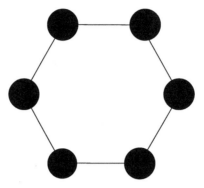

Figure 1.2. A schematic of a multiple-population parallel GA. Each circle represents a simple GA, and there is (infrequent) communication between the populations.

into geographically-separated subpopulations with migration between any two populations, so the parallel GAs are also known as "island" parallel GAs. If migration is restricted between neighboring populations, the population model is called "stepping stone", but we will not distinguish between the two in this book.

Some have argued that multiple-deme GAs are a closer analogy to natural populations than the simple GAs with a single population, and observations of phenomena that occur in natural populations are common. For instance, Cohoon et al. (1987, 1991) noted similarities between the evolution process in a parallel GA and the theory of punctuated equilibria (Elredge & Gould, 1972). This theory suggests that most of the time there are no significant changes in a population (i.e., it is in equilibrium), but some events trigger rapid evolutionary changes. Cohoon et al. observed that migration can be such an event. Another example is the study of Sumida et al. (1990) on the performance of a multi-deme GA, which was motivated by Wright's (1932) shifting balance model. In essence, Wright's model describes small populations that find different locally-optimal solutions. The populations send emigrants, that have the effect of attracting the other subpopulations to their solutions, possibly crossing valleys of low fitness that would have remained unexplored otherwise. This additional exploration may discover even better solutions.

Although the biological implications are interesting, the focus of this book is on the engineering of GAs. From this point of view, parallel GAs with multiple demes are attractive because the size of the demes is smaller than the population used by a serial GA, and therefore we would expect them to converge faster if we assign each to a separate processor.

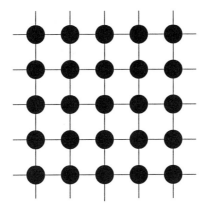

Figure 1.3. A schematic of a fine-grained parallel GA. This class of parallel GAs has one spatially-distributed population, and it can be implemented very efficiently on massively parallel computers.

However, when we compare the performance of the serial and the parallel algorithms, we must also consider the quality of the solutions found in each case: while it is true that smaller demes converge faster, it is also true that the quality of the solution might be poorer. This tradeoff will be examined in detail in the rest of the book.

The third type of parallel GAs are fine-grained algorithms. They consist of a single spatially-structured population (see Figure 1.3). The population structure is usually a two-dimensional rectangular grid, and there is one individual per grid point. Ideally, there is one processor per individual, so the evaluation of fitness is performed simultaneously for all the individuals. Selection and mating are restricted to a small neighborhood around each individual. The neighborhoods overlap, so that eventually the good traits of a superior individual can spread to the entire population. This class of parallel GAs is also sometimes called "diffusion-model" GAs, because the spread of good traits to the population is analogous to the random diffusion of particles in some fluid. This class of parallel GAs is also known as "cellular GAs", because it is a class of cellular automata with stochastic transition rules (Whitley, 1993a; Tomassini, 1993). Fine-grained GAs are well suited for massively parallel SIMD computers, which execute the same single instruction on all the processors, but it is also possible to implement them very efficiently on coarse-grain MIMD computers (Hart, 1994; Hart et al., 1996). This type of parallel GAs has not been studied as much as the others, but some important results are summarized in Chapter 8.

It is important to emphasize that while the master-slave method does not generally affect the behavior of the algorithm, the last two methods change the way the GA works. For example, selection in master-slave GAs takes into account all the population, but in the other two parallel GAs, selection considers only a subset of individuals. Also, in the master-slave, any two individuals in the population can mate (i.e., there is panmictic mating), but in the other methods, mating is restricted to individuals that are geographically close.

The behavior of GAs with spatially-distributed populations is interesting, regardless of their implementation on serial or parallel computers (Gordon & Whitley, 1993; Hart, 1994; Punch, 1998). Having a geographically-distributed population may have some algorithmic benefits that are independent of the efficiency gains obtained from using multiple processors (e.g., (Mühlenbein, 1991; Whitley & Starkweather, 1990; Davidor, 1993; Calégari, 1999)). In fact, most of this book is about modeling the effect of the algorithms' parameters. Once the models have been found, we use them to optimize the execution time of the algorithms.

The final method to parallelize GAs combines multiple demes with master-slave or fine-grained GAs. We call this class of algorithms hierarchical parallel GAs, because at a higher level they are multiple-deme algorithms with single-population parallel GAs (either master-slave or fine-grained) at the lower level. A hierarchical parallel GAs combines the benefits of its components, and it has the potential of better performance than any of them alone. The hierarchical algorithms are very well suited to be implemented on symmetric multi-processors. Chapter 8 shows how to integrate the previous results to design hierarchical parallel GAs to minimize the execution time.

There are synchronous and asynchronous versions of each type of parallel GA. In the synchronous algorithms, the multiple processors always deal with individuals of the same generation, and there is some form of communication to synchronize the processes. This means that the faster processors have to wait for the slower ones before continuing to the next generation. In the asynchronous cases, the processors proceed at their own pace, and processor idle times are reduced greatly. However, asynchronous algorithms behave differently than the synchronous types, and it is difficult to predict or replicate results, because communications occur at random times.

This book deals mainly with synchronous algorithms, because their behavior is more tractable, and most of the literature deals with this type. In practice, they are also very efficient, even if some processors are idle some of the time. However, we must recognize that asynchronous algorithms may be more efficient in most cases.

We should point out that there is no need of specialized hardware to implement parallel GAs. In general, the communication requirements of all the algorithms are low, and inexpensive hardware such as Beowulf-style clusters (Sterling, 1998; Bennett III et al., 1999; Gwo et al., 2000) or Web-based computations can be very practical (Nangsue & Conry, 1998; Chong, 1999). In fact, since some of the algorithms have interesting properties regardless of their implementation, simulating them on a serial processor can be beneficial in some cases.

3 SUMMARY

Genetic algorithms are effective to solve many practical problems, but in some cases, they may take a long time to reach an acceptable solution. GAs are easy to implement on parallel computers, and indeed, parallel GAs are popular, but they are controlled by many parameters that are not well understood. The purpose of this book is to explore the effects of the parameters on the search quality and efficiency of parallel GAs, and provide guidelines on how to choose appropriate values for a particular situation.

This chapter presented a brief description of GAs and some concepts that will be used in the remainder of the book. In particular, the next chapter uses the concepts of partitions and schemata to develop a model that relates the quality of the solution reached by a simple GA with the size of its population. This chapter also outlined the different types of parallel GAs that are explored in the rest of the book.

Chapter 2

THE GAMBLER'S RUIN PROBLEM AND POPULATION SIZING

As we saw in the previous chapter, genetic algorithms operate on a population of individuals that encode solutions of a problem that we want to solve. One of the most important decisions needed to use a GA is to determine the number of individuals in the population. However, the question of how to choose an adequate population size for a particular domain is difficult, and has puzzled GA practitioners for a long time. If the population is too small, there might not be an adequate supply of building blocks, and it would be difficult to identify good solutions. On the other hand, if the population is too large, the GA would waste time processing unnecessary individuals, which may result in unacceptably slow performance. The challenge consists on finding a population size that is large enough to permit a correct exploration of the search space, and that does not waste computational resources. We face the same population-sizing problem when we use parallel GAs, and therefore, the results of this chapter are important to our quest for efficient parallel GAs.

This chapter presents a model to predict the convergence quality of genetic algorithms based on the size of their population. The model is based on an analogy between the selection mechanism in GAs and one-dimensional random walks. Using the solution to a classic random walk problem (the gambler's ruin), the model naturally incorporates previous knowledge about the initial supply of building blocks and the correct selection of the best BB over its competitors. The result is an accurate relation between the size of the population with the desired quality of the solution, as well as the problem size and difficulty.

The chapter is largely based on a paper by Harik, Cantú-Paz, Goldberg, and Miller (1997), and is organized as follows. It begins by presenting the facetwise decomposition that guides this work and a brief discussion of some previous studies on population sizing. Section 2 revisits in detail a model that describes the probability of choosing correctly between two competing individuals. This pairwise decision probability is an integral part of the population sizing model presented in Section 3. Section 4 confirms the accuracy of the model with results of experiments on problems of varying difficulty. Section 5 discusses how to extend the model to account for explicit noise in the fitness of the individuals, and Section 6 extends the model to consider different selection types. The chapter concludes with a brief summary.

1   BACKGROUND

Over the years, researchers and practitioners have noticed that the population size is a big factor in the convergence quality of GAs and the duration of their run. Unfortunately, there are only a handful of studies that guide users to choose adequate population sizes. This section reviews some of these studies, but first it describes the decomposition that guides our study of GAs.

1.1   DECOMPOSING THE PROBLEM

Despite their operational simplicity, GAs are complex non-linear algorithms. To have any hope of understanding and designing GAs we need to approach them as we do with other difficult engineering tasks: decompose the problem into tractable sub-problems, solve the sub-problems, and integrate the partial solutions. Goldberg (1991) proposed the following facetwise decomposition as a guide to study GAs:

1. Know what the GA is processing: building blocks (BBs)

2. Solve problems tractable by BBs

3. Supply enough BBs in the initial population

4. Ensure the growth of necessary BBs

5. Mix the BBs properly

6. Decide well among competing BBs

   Recall from the previous chapter that BBs are low-order highly-fit schemata, and that we label as correct BBs those schemata in the lowest-order partition that consistently lead to the global optimum. Other schemata in the same partition are labeled as incorrect, even if they have a high average fitness.

   The gambler's ruin model described later in this chapter involves two of the six points mentioned above: the initial supply and the decision process between competing BBs. The result is what elsewhere (Goldberg, 1996b) has been called a *little model*: it does not attempt to describe the effect of all possible parameters on the search. Instead, the model focuses only on the supply and decision issues and describes a practical relation between population size and solution quality. Although the model excludes the important effects of mixing and growth of BBs, the result is very accurate, and it can be used to guide the design of faster and more reliable GAs.

Previous estimates of adequate population sizes consider only the supply of BBs or the decision-making among competing BBs. The remainder of this section reviews some of these previous studies.

1.2 SUPPLY MODELS

Before selection and recombination can act on the BBs, the GA first needs to have an adequate supply. When BBs are abundant, it is likely that the GA will choose and combine them correctly to reach a good solution; conversely, when BBs are scarce, the chances of the GA converging to a good solution are low.

The first supply model simply considers the number of BBs present in the initial random population. The probability that a single building block of size k is generated randomly is $1/2^k$ for binary domains, and therefore the initial supply of BBs can be estimated as

$$x_0 = \frac{n}{2^k}. \tag{2.1}$$

This simple supply equation suggests that domains with short BBs—and thus with more BBs in the initial population—need smaller population sizes than domains with longer BBs.

Another way of relating the size of the population with the expected performance of the GA is to count the number of schemata processed by the GA. Holland (1975) estimated that a randomly initialized population of size n contains $O(n^3)$ schemata. Holland used the term *implicit parallelism* to denote this fact, and it has become one of the common arguments on why GAs work well.[1] Goldberg (1989a) rederived this estimate in two steps that are reproduced below: (1) compute the number of schemata in one string, and then (2) multiply it by the population size.

The number of schemata of length l_s or less in one random binary string of length l is $2^{l_s-1}(l - l_s + 1)$. The schema length l_s is chosen such

---

[1]Do not confuse the concept of "implicit parallelism" that refers to the partial evaluation of multiple schemata from the fitness of a single individual with the "explicit" parallel implementations of GAs on multiple processors. These concepts are completely unrelated.

that the schemata survive crossover and mutation with a given constant probability. It is likely that low-order schemata will be duplicated in large populations, so to avoid overestimating the number of schemata, pick a population size $n = 2^{l_s/2}$, so that on average half of the schemata are of higher order than $l_s/2$ and half are of lower order. Counting only the higher order ones gives a lower bound on the number of schemata in the population as $n_s \geq n(l - l_s + 1)2^{l_s-2}$. Since $n = 2^{l_s/2}$ this becomes $n_s = \frac{(l-l_s+1)n^3}{4}$, which is $O(n^3)$.

In a different study, Goldberg (1989b) computed the expected number of unique schemata in a random population, and used this quantity together with an estimate of the convergence time to find the optimal population size that maximizes the rate of schema processing. Goldberg considered serial and parallel fitness evaluations, and his results suggest that high schema turnover is promoted with small populations in serial GAs and with large populations in parallel.

Reeves (1993) investigated the use of GAs with very small populations. He proposed to size the population to ensure that with a certain (high) probability at least one allele is present at each locus. In principle, this allows crossover to reach every possible point in the search space. Reeves presented calculations for alphabets of arbitrary cardinalities, and showed that relatively small populations are required to satisfy his criterion. However, the calculations ignored the length of the BBs, and may recommend populations that are too small to solve problems with long BBs.

More recently, Mühlenbein and Schlierkamp-Voosen (1994) derived an expression for the smallest population size that the GA needs to converge to the optimum with high probability. Their analysis is based on additive fitness functions, and their study focuses on the simplest function of this type: the one-max, which we also use later in this chapter. They conjectured that the optimal population size depends on the initial supply of the desired alleles, on the size of the problem, and on the selection intensity. Our study also considers the effect of these variables on the population size, and shows the relationships between those parameters. Later, Cvetković and Mühlenbein (1994) empirically determined that, for the one-max, the population size is directly proportional to the square root of the size of the problem, and it is inversely proportional to the square root of the proportion of correct alleles in the initial population. Our results are also based on additive fitness functions, and are consistent with their experimental fit on the problem size, but indicate that, in general, the population size is inversely proportional to the proportion of correct BBs present initially (not to the square root).

1.3 DECISION MODELS

The second aspect of population sizing involves selecting better partial solutions. Holland (1973, 1975) recognized that the issue of choosing between BBs (and not between complete strings) can be recast as a two-armed bandit problem, a well-known problem in statistical decision theory. The problem consists in choosing the arm with the highest payoff of a two-armed slot machine, at the same time that payoff information is collected. This classic problem is a concrete example of the tradeoff between exploring the sample space and exploiting the information already gathered. Holland's work assumes an idealization of the GA as a cluster of interconnected 2-armed bandits, so his result relating the expected loss and the number of trials can be directly applied to schema processing. Although Holland's calculations are based on an idealization, his results give an optimistic bound on the allocation of trials on a real GA.

Around the same time, De Jong (1975) recognized the importance of noise in the decision process and proposed an estimate of the population size based on the signal and noise characteristics of the problem. Unfortunately, he did not use his estimate in the remaining of his groundbreaking empirical study, and this result has remained unverified and ignored by many.

Goldberg and Rudnick (1991) gave the first population sizing estimate based on the variance of fitness. Later, Goldberg, Deb, and Clark (1992) developed a conservative bound on the convergence quality of GAs. Their model is based on deciding correctly between the best BB in a partition and its closest competitor, while the decision process is clouded by collateral noise coming from the other partitions.

The result of Goldberg, Deb and Clark's investigation is a population sizing equation that for binary alphabets and ignoring external sources of noise is:

$$n = 2c(\alpha)2^k m' \frac{\sigma_M^2}{d^2}, \tag{2.2}$$

where $c(\alpha)$ is the square of the ordinate of a unit normal distribution where the probability equals α; α is the probability of failure; k is the order of the BB; m' is one less than the number of BBs in a string (m); σ_M^2 is the average fitness variance of the partition that is being considered; and d is the fitness difference between the best and second best BBs. The next section explains some of this terms in detail.

Goldberg et al.'s model conservatively approximates the behavior of the GA by assuming that if the wrong BBs were selected in the first generation, the GA would be unable to recover from the error, and it

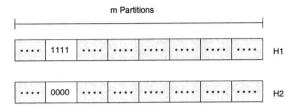

Figure 2.1.   Two competing building blocks of order four.

would converge to the wrong solution. Likewise, the model assumes that if the decisions were correct in the first generation, the GA would converge to the right solution. This study is a direct extension of the work by Goldberg et al. The main difference between the current model and theirs is that we do not approximate the behavior of the GA by the outcome of the first generation.

2   DECIDING WELL BETWEEN TWO BBs

The role of selection in GAs is to decide which individuals survive to form the next generation. The selection mechanism is supposed to choose those individuals that have the correct BBs and to eliminate the others, but sometimes the wrong individuals are chosen. To understand why this may occur, this section reviews the calculations of Goldberg et al. (1992) of the probability of deciding well between an individual with the best BB and another individual with the second best BB in a partition. The critical idea is to focus on one partition, and to consider the fitness contributions from the other partitions as noise that interferes in the decision process.

Consider a competition between an individual i_1 that contains the optimal BB in a partition, H_1, and an individual i_2 with the second best BB, H_2. This is illustrated in Figure 2.1. The probability of deciding correctly between these two individuals is the probability that the fitness of i_1 (f_1) is greater than the fitness of i_2 (f_2) or equivalently the probability that $f_1 - f_2 > 0$.

Figure 2.2 illustrates the distributions of the fitness of individuals that contain H_1 and H_2. The distance between the mean fitness of H_1 ($\bar{f}_{H_1}$) and the mean fitness of H_2 ($\bar{f}_{H_2}$) is denoted by d. Assuming that the fitness is an additive function of the fitness contribution of all the partitions in the problem, we may consider that the fitness of H_1 and H_2 have a normal distribution (because the fitness contribution of each partition is a random variable, and the central limit theorem states that the sum of random variables is normally distributed).

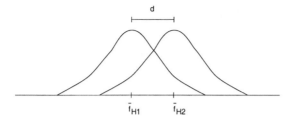

Figure 2.2.   Fitness distributions for two competing individuals.

Since the fitness distributions of i_1 and i_2 are normal, the distribution of $f_1 - f_2$ is itself normal and has known properties: the mean is the difference of the individual means, and the variance is the sum of the individual variances,

$$f_1 - f_2 \sim N(\bar{f}_{H_1} - \bar{f}_{H_2}, \sigma^2_{H_1} + \sigma^2_{H_2}). \tag{2.3}$$

Substituting $d = \bar{f}_{H_1} - \bar{f}_{H_2}$ in the expression above and normalizing, the probability of making the correct decision on a single trial is

$$p = \Phi\left(\frac{d}{\sqrt{\sigma^2_{H_1} + \sigma^2_{H_2}}}\right), \tag{2.4}$$

where Φ is the cumulative distribution function (CDF) of a normal distribution with zero mean and unit standard distribution.

To calculate the variance of H_1 and H_2, we follow Goldberg et al. (1992), and assume that the fitness function is the sum of m independent subfunctions, F_i, each of the same size, k, of the most deceptive partition. Under these assumptions, the overall fitness variance is

$$\sigma^2_F = \sum_{i=1}^{m} \sigma^2_{F_i}. \tag{2.5}$$

For domains where the m partitions are uniformly scaled (equally weighted), the average BB variance (denoted by σ^2_{bb}) is simply $\sigma^2_{F_i}$. In this case, the total noise coming from the $m' = m - 1$ partitions that are not competing directly is $\sigma^2_F = m'\sigma^2_{bb}$. Therefore, the probability of making the right choice in a single trial in a problem with m independent and equally-scaled partitions becomes

$$p = \Phi\left(\frac{d}{\sqrt{2m'\sigma_{bb}}}\right). \tag{2.6}$$

Figure 2.3.   The bounded one-dimensional space of the gambler's ruin problem.

Goldberg et al. (1992) used this probability to create the first model that relates the size of the population with the quality of decisions. Their model showed how to incorporate the effect of collateral noise into the population-sizing question, and their paper describes how to estimate the parameters necessary to calculate p. In the next section, that knowledge about noise and decision-making at the BB level will be unified quite naturally with the knowledge about the initial supply of BBs.

3   THE GAMBLER'S RUIN MODEL

The gambler's ruin problem is a classical example of random walks, which are mathematical tools that can be used to predict the outcome of certain stochastic processes. The most basic random walk deals with a particle that moves randomly on a one-dimensional space. The probability that the particle moves to the left or to the right is known, and it remains constant for the entire experiment. The size of the step is also constant, and sometimes the movement of the particle is restricted by placing barriers at some points in the space. For our purposes, we consider a one-dimensional space bounded by two absorbing barriers that capture the particle once it reaches them.

In the gambler's ruin problem, the capital of a gambler is represented by the position, x, of a particle on a one-dimensional space, as depicted in Figure 2.3. Initially, the particle is positioned at $x_0 = a$, where a represents the gambler's starting capital. The gambler plays against an opponent that has an initial capital of $n - a$, and there are absorbing boundaries at $x = 0$ (representing the gambler's bankruptcy) and at $x = n$ (representing winning all the opponent's money). At each step in the game, the gambler has a chance p of increasing his capital by one unit and a probability $q = 1 - p$ of loosing one unit. The object of the game is to reach the boundary at $x = n$. The probability of success depends on the initial capital and on the probability of winning a particular trial.

The connection between selection in GAs and the gambler's ruin problem was first proposed by Harik et al. (1997), and appears naturally when we assume that partitions are independent and we concentrate on only one of them. The particle's position on the one-dimensional space, x, represents the number of copies of the correct BBs in the population. The absorbing barriers at $x = 0$ and $x = n$ represent convergence to the wrong and to the correct solutions, respectively. The initial position of the particle, x_0, is the expected number of copies of the correct BB in a randomly initialized population, which in a binary domain and considering BBs of order k is $x_0 = \frac{n}{2^k}$.

There are some assumptions that we need to make to use the gambler's ruin problem to predict the quality of the solutions of the GA. The gambler's ruin model considers that decisions in a GA occur one at a time until all the n individuals in the population converge to the same value. In other words, in the model there is no explicit notion of generations, and the outcome of each decision is to win or loose one copy of the optimal BB. We also need the conservative assumption that all competitions occur between strings that represent the best and the second best BBs in a partition, and therefore, the probability of gaining a copy of the best BB is given by p (Equation 2.6).

The calculation of p implicitly assumed that the GA uses pairwise tournament selection (two strings compete), but adjustments for other selection schemes are possible, as we shall see in a later section. The analogy between GAs and the gambler's ruin problem also assumes that the only source of BBs is the random initialization of the population. This assumption implies that mutation and crossover do not create or destroy significant numbers of BBs. The boundaries of the random walk are absorbing; this means that once a partition contains n copies of the correct BB it cannot loose one, and likewise, when the correct BB disappears from a partition there is no way of recovering it. We recognize that the gambler's ruin model is a simplification of a real GA, but experimental results suggest that is it a reasonable one.

As we discussed above, the GA succeeds when there are n copies of the correct BB in the partition of interest. A well-known result in the random walk literature is that the probability that the particle will eventually be captured by the absorbing barrier at $x = n$ is (Feller, 1966)

$$P_{bb} = \frac{1 - \left(\frac{q}{p}\right)^{x_0}}{1 - \left(\frac{q}{p}\right)^{n}}. \tag{2.7}$$

From this equation, it is relatively easy to find an expression for the population size. First, note that by definition $p > 1 - p$ (because the mean fitness of the best BB is greater than the mean fitness of the second best), and that x_0 is usually small compared to the population size. Therefore, for increasing values of n the denominator in Equation 2.7

approaches 1 very quickly, and it can be ignored in the calculations. Substituting the initial supply of BBs ($x_0 = n/2^k$), P_{bb} may be approximated as

$$P_{bb} \approx 1 - \left(\frac{1-p}{p}\right)^{n/2^k}. \tag{2.8}$$

We measure the quality of the solutions as the number of partitions Q that converge to the correct BB. Since we assume that the m partitions are independent of each other, the expected number of partitions with the correct BB at the end of a run is $E(Q) = mP_{bb}$. Assuming that we are interested in finding a solution with an average of $\hat{Q}$ partitions correct, we can solve $P_{bb} = \frac{\hat{Q}}{m}$ for n to obtain the following population-sizing equation:

$$n = \frac{2^k \ln(\alpha)}{\ln\left(\frac{1-p}{p}\right)}, \tag{2.9}$$

where $\alpha = 1 - \frac{\hat{Q}}{m}$ is the probability of failure. To observe more clearly the relations between the population size and the domain-dependent variables involved, we may expand p and write the last equation in terms of the signal, the noise, and the number of partitions in the problem. First, approximate p using the first two terms of the power series expansion for the normal distribution as (Abramowitz & Stegun, 1972):

$$p = \frac{1}{2} + \frac{1}{\sqrt{2\pi}}z, \tag{2.10}$$

where $z = d/(\sigma_{bb}\sqrt{2m'})$. Substituting this approximation for p into Equation 2.9 results in

$$n = 2^k \ln(\alpha)/\ln\left(\frac{1 - \frac{z\sqrt{2}}{\sqrt{\pi}}}{1 + \frac{z\sqrt{2}}{\sqrt{\pi}}}\right). \tag{2.11}$$

Since z tends to be a small number, $\ln(1 \pm \frac{z\sqrt{2}}{\sqrt{\pi}})$ may be approximated as $\pm\frac{z\sqrt{2}}{\sqrt{\pi}}$. Using these approximations and substituting the value of z into the equation above gives

$$n = -2^{k-1}\ln(\alpha)\frac{\sigma_{bb}\sqrt{\pi m'}}{d}. \tag{2.12}$$

This rough approximation makes more clear the relations between some of the variables that determine when a problem is harder than others. It quantifies many intuitive notions that practitioners have about problem difficulty for GAs. For example, problems with long BBs (large k) are more difficult to solve than problems with short BBs, because long BBs are scarcer in a randomly initialized population. Furthermore, the equation shows that the required population size is inversely proportional to the signal-to-noise ratio. Intuitively, problems with a high variability are hard because it is difficult to detect the signal coming from the good solutions when the interference from not-so-good solutions is high. Similarly, longer problems (larger m) are more difficult than problems with a few partitions because there are more sources of noise. However, the GA scales very well to the problem size: the equation shows that the required population grows as the square root of the size of the problem.

4 EXPERIMENTAL VERIFICATION

This section verifies that the gambler's ruin model predicts accurately the quality of the solutions reached by simple GAs. The experiments reported in this section use additively-decomposable functions of varying difficulty, which will be used to test the parallel GA models presented in later chapters. The population sizes required to solve the test problems vary from a few tens to a few thousands, demonstrating that the predictions of the model scale well to the problem's difficulty.

All the results in this chapter are the average over 100 independent runs of a simple generational GA. The GA used pairwise tournament selection without replacement. The crossover operator was chosen according to the order of the BBs of each problem, and is specified in each subsection below. In all the experiments, the mutation probability was set to zero, because the model considers that the only source of diversity is the initial random population. Each run was terminated when all the individuals in the population are the same (which is possible because the mutation rate was zero), and we report the percentage of partitions that converged to the correct value. The predictions of the gambler's ruin model were calculated with Equation 2.7.

4.1 ONE-MAX

The one-max problem is probably the most frequently-used test function in research on genetic algorithms because of its simplicity. This function measures the fitness of an individual as the number of bits set to one in the chromosome: $F = \sum_{i=1}^{l} x_i$, where $x_i \in \{0, 1\}$ represents the i-th bit in the chromosome. The one-max is a very easy problem for GAs because there is no isolation or deception and the BBs are short. The supply of

BBs is no problem either, because a randomly initialized population has on average 50% of the correct BBs.

In this function, the order of the BBs is $k = 1$. The fitness difference is $d = 1$ because a correct partition contributes one to the fitness and an incorrect partition contributes nothing. The variance may be calculated as $\sigma_{bb}^2 = (1 - 0)/4 = 0.25$ (see the paper by Goldberg, Deb, and Clark (1992) for a discussion on how to approximate or bound σ_{bb}^2). The first set of experiments uses strings with $m = 100$ bits. Substituting these values into Equation 2.6 gives that the probability of choosing correctly between two competing BBs in this problem is $p = 0.5565$. The length of the BBs is one, so crossover cannot disrupt them, and therefore, we chose to use uniform crossover for this function as it mixes BBs quite effectively. The probability of applying crossover was set to 1.0, and the probability of exchanging each bit by uniform crossover was set to 0.5. The second set of experiments used strings with $m = 500$ bits.

Figure 2.4 reports the results of the experiments with the one-max function along with the predictions. In this figure, the bold line is the prediction of the gambler's ruin model and the dotted line is the experimental results. The thin line is the prediction of the population sizing model of Goldberg et al. (1992). As expected, in the longer problem, the population size required to find solutions of equivalent quality is greater than in the shorter problem.

The gambler's ruin model predicts the outcome of the experiments for the 100 and 500-bit functions quite accurately. However, in the 500-bit function the match is not as close as in the 100-bit case. The reason for this small discrepancy may be that the theory only considers one partition at a time and it assumes that decisions for one partition are independent of all the others. To achieve this independence, crossover must distribute BBs completely at random across all the individuals in the population.[2] However, it would not be practical to reach this perfect distribution, because many rounds of crossover would be necessary in every generation. The problem of inadequate mixing is aggravated as longer strings are used. The predictions of the model should be much more accurate for algorithms such as PBIL (Baluja, 1994), UMDA (Mühlenbein & Paaß, 1996), or the compact GA (Harik, Lobo, & Goldberg, 1998), which treat each bit independently and do not suffer from the inadequate mixing problem described here.

---

[2]This state is called linkage equilibrium, and it is well known that crossover moves the population towards it (Qi & Palmieri, 1993).

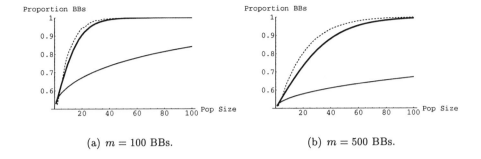

(a) $m = 100$ BBs.   (b) $m = 500$ BBs.

Figure 2.4. Experiments and theoretical predictions of the proportion of correct BBs on 100-bit and 500-bit one-max functions. The prediction of the random walk model is in bold, the experimental results are the dotted line, and the previous decision-based model is the thin line.

Additional experiments reported by Harik et al. (1997, 1999) with non-uniformly scaled one-max problems suggest that the gambler's ruin model is also accurate in those cases.

4.2   DECEPTIVE FUNCTIONS

The next two sets of experiments use fully-deceptive trap functions. Deceptive trap functions are used in many studies of GAs because their difficulty is well understood and it can be regulated easily (Deb & Goldberg, 1993).

The first deceptive test function used in the experiments is based on the 4-bit trap function depicted in Figure 2.5, which was also used by Goldberg, Deb, and Clark (1992) in their study of population sizing. As in the one-max, the value of this function depends on the number of bits set to one, but in this case the fitness increases with more bits set to zero until it reaches a local (deceptive) optimum. The global maximum of the function occurs precisely at the opposite extreme where all four bits are set to one, so an algorithm cannot use any partial information to find it. More formally, we can say that all schemata of order $k \leq 3$ with at least one fixed position $\mathsf{F} = 0$ have a higher average fitness than schemata where the same fixed position is $\mathsf{F} = 1$. This misleads the GA to the suboptimal solution with all zeroes. The shortest schemata that leads to the global optimum is of order $k = 4$, and all its fixed positions are $\mathsf{F} = 1$ (this is the correct BB). The difference between the global and the deceptive maxima is $d = 1$, and the fitness variance (σ_{bb}^2) is 1.215. The test function is formed by concatenating $m = 20$ copies of the trap function for a total string length of 80 bits: $F = \sum_{i=1}^{20} f_i$, where f_i is defined in Figure 2.5. The probability of making the right

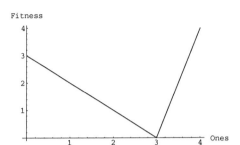

Figure 2.5.   A 4-bit deceptive function.

decision between two individuals with the best and the second best BBs is $p = 0.5585$. We can construct more difficult deceptive functions by using more bits in the basin of the deceptive optimum, or by reducing the fitness difference between the global and deceptive maxima.

Many optimizers have problems to solve trap functions, because they tend to climb to the deceptive peak, but the experiments show that GAs with properly-sized populations can solve trap problems. For these problems, we expect to use larger population sizes than with the one-max for two reasons: (1) the BBs are scarcer in the initial population, because they are longer; and (2) the signal to noise ratio is smaller, making the decision between the best and the second best BBs more difficult.

To solve the trap functions, tight linkage was used (i.e., the bits that define each trap function are positioned next to each other in the chromosome), although there are algorithms such as the messy GA (Goldberg et al., 1989) and its relatives (Goldberg et al., 1993; Kargupta, 1996; Harik & Goldberg, 1996) that are able to find tight linkages automatically. Other modern GAs that explicitly identify BBs and treat them independently, such as the extended compact GA (Harik, 1999) and the Bayesian optimization algorithm (Pelikan et al., 1999) also benefit from the gambler's ruin theory.

The experiments with the 4-bit trap function use two-point crossover to avoid the excessive disruption that uniform crossover would cause on the longer BBs. As before, the crossover probability is set to 1.0, and there is no mutation. Figure 2.6 presents the prediction of the percentage of BBs correct at the end of the run along with the results from the experiments. The bold line is the prediction of the random walk model and the thin line is the prediction of the previous decision-only model. Note that the convergence quality for small population sizes is

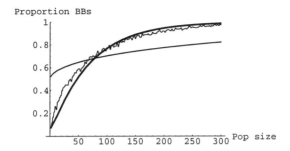

Figure 2.6. Theoretical predictions and experimental results for a 4-bit deceptive function with 20 BBs. The model (in bold) approximates well the experimental results (dotted). The thin line is the previous decision-making model.

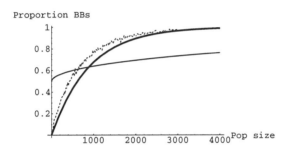

Figure 2.7. Theoretical predictions and experimental results (dotted line) for a 8-bit deceptive function with 10 BBs. The predictions of the gambler's ruin model are in bold, and the previous decision-making model is plotted with a thin line.

dominated by the initial supply of BBs, and, as expected, the previous model is not accurate in that region.

The second deceptive test function is formed by concatenating $m = 10$ copies of an 8-bit fully-deceptive trap. The 8-bit trap is similar to the 4-bit used above with a signal difference $d = 1$, but the fitness variance is $\sigma_{bb}^2 = 2.1804$. The higher variance and longer BBs make this function more difficult than the 4-bit problem, so larger populations are expected in this case. One-point crossover was used for this function because the longer BBs are more likely to be disrupted by crossover. The crossover probability was again set to 1.0 and there is no mutation. Figure 2.7 shows the results for this problem.

Additional experiments reported elsewhere (Harik et al., 1999) suggest that the gambler's ruin model is also accurate on functions composed of deceptive traps defined over overlapping substrings.

5 NOISE AND POPULATION SIZING

Genetic algorithms are being used increasingly to solve problems where the fitness of an individual cannot be determined exactly due to noise in the evaluation function. The noise may come from an inherently noisy domain or from a noisy approximation of an excessively expensive fitness function. This section examines how this explicit fitness noise affects the size of the population.

Following Goldberg, Deb, and Clark (1992) the noisy fitness F' of an individual can be described as

$$F' = F + N, \tag{2.13}$$

where F is the true fitness of an individual and N is the noise present in the evaluation. The effect of the added noise is to increase the fitness variance of the population, making it more difficult to choose correctly between two competing individuals. Therefore, the one-on-one decision-making probability (Equation 2.6) has to be modified to include the effect of explicit noise; then, it may be used to find the required population size as was done in Section 3.

Assuming that the noise is normally distributed as $N(0, \sigma_N^2)$, the fitness variance becomes $\sigma_F^2 + \sigma_N^2$. Therefore, the probability of choosing correctly between an individual with the optimal building block and an individual with the second best BB in a noisy environment is

$$p = \Phi\left(\frac{d}{\sqrt{\sigma_{H_1}^2 + \sigma_{H_2}^2 + 2\sigma_N^2}}\right). \tag{2.14}$$

In the case of uniformly-scaled problems this becomes (Miller, 1997)

$$p = \Phi\left(\frac{d}{\sqrt{2(m'\sigma_{bb}^2 + \sigma_N^2)}}\right). \tag{2.15}$$

Using this form of p and the same procedure used to obtain Equation 2.11 results in the following population sizing equation for noisy domains:

$$n = -2^{k-1}\ln(\alpha)\frac{\sqrt{\pi m'\sigma_{bb}^2 + \sigma_N^2}}{d}. \tag{2.16}$$

The one-max problem was used to test the predictions of the gambler's ruin model (Equation 2.7) using the decision probability given by Equation 2.15. The experiments used a 100-bit problem with uniform crossover and no mutation. The fitness variance is $\sigma_F^2 = m\sigma_{bb}^2 = 25$ and

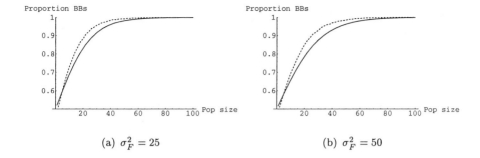

(a) $\sigma_F^2 = 25$ (b) $\sigma_F^2 = 50$

Figure 2.8. Theoretical and experimental results for 100-bit one-max functions with different levels of added noise. The noise is constant for each set of experiments, and the population size ranges from 2 to 100.

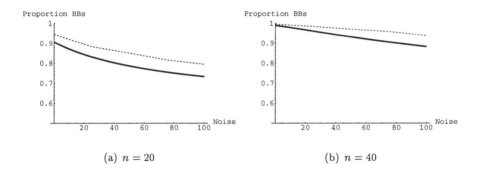

(a) $n = 20$ (b) $n = 40$

Figure 2.9. Theoretical and experimental results for 100-bit one-max functions varying the noise levels from $\sigma_F^2 = 0$ to 100. The population size remained constant for each set of experiments.

the experiments were run for $\sigma_N^2 = \sigma_F^2$ and $\sigma_N^2 = 2\sigma_F^2$. Figure 2.8 displays the average proportion of partitions that converge correctly (taken over 100 independent runs at each population size) for each noise level. The figure shows that the predictions match well the empirical results.

The effect of the increasing noise in the quality of convergence may be observed more clearly in Figure 2.9. In this set of experiments, the population size was held constant while the noise increased. The gambler's ruin model correctly predicts that additional noise causes the GA to reach solutions of lower quality, and although the predictions are not exact, the model is conservative and may be used to estimate the required population size.

6 THE EFFECT OF SELECTION PRESSURE

Besides of the population size, an important factor in the convergence quality of GAs is the selection scheme. After all, the selection mechanism is the part of the GA making the decisions we discussed in the previous sections. Only tournament selection is considered here, but the results may be extrapolated to other selection methods with known constant selection intensities (see Bäck (1994b), Miller and Goldberg (1996)). A different analysis would be necessary for schemes such as proportional selection that do not have a constant selection pressure.

The selection pressure of tournament selection increases with the size of the tournaments, which is denoted by s. To analyze the effect on the population size, we assume conservatively that the correct BB competes against $s - 1$ copies of the second best BB. As larger tournaments are considered, the probability of making the wrong decision increases proportionately to s; thus, we approximate the probability of making the right decision as $1/s$. In reality, this probability is higher than $1/s$ since a tournament might involve more than one copy of the best BB—especially as the run progresses and the proportion of correct BBs increases. However, $1/s$ is a good initial approximation as the experimental results suggest.

The increasing difficulty of decision-making as the tournament size increases can be accounted for as a contraction in the signal that the GA is trying to detect. Setting the new signal to

$$d' = d + \Phi^{-1}\left(\frac{1}{s}\right)\sigma_{bb}, \qquad (2.17)$$

where $\Phi^{-1}(1/s)$ is the ordinate of a unit normal distribution where the CDF equals $1/s$, we can compute a new probability of deciding well using d' instead of d in Equation 2.6. Note that the second term in the equation above is negative, so with larger tournaments the signal would becomes smaller and the population larger. Others have also observed that the population size increases with the selection pressure (e.g., Mühlenbein and Schlierkamp-Voosen (1994), Bäck (1996), Ochoa et al. (2000)).

Experiments were performed using a 100-bit one-max function and tournament sizes of 2, 4, and 8. The experimental results are plotted in Figure 2.10 with dotted lines along with the theoretical predictions. The leftmost plot corresponds to a tournament size $s = 2$, the middle one to $s = 4$, and the rightmost to $s = 8$. Once again, the model is a good predictor for the proportion of BBs correct at the end of the run.

The result of this section has consequences on the design of parallel genetic algorithms, not only because the choice of selection affects the population size, but also because some implementations of parallel GAs

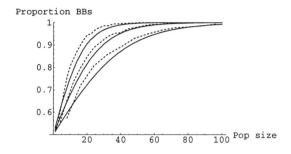

Figure 2.10. Predictions and experimental results for a 100-bit one-max function varying the selection intensity. From left to right: $s = 2, 4, 8$.

may change the selection pressure. Often, these effects on the selection pressure are implicit in the implementation and may be unintended. As such, it is easy to ignore them, and the user may erroneously choose a population size that is too small to reach the desired solution. There are further discussions about the implementation's impact on the selection pressure in Chapters 3 and 7.

7   SUMMARY

This chapter presented a solution to a long-standing problem in genetic algorithms: how to determine an adequate population size to reach a solution of a particular quality. The model is based on a random walk where the position of a particle on a bounded one-dimensional space represents the number of copies of the correct BBs in the population. The probability that the particle will be absorbed by the boundaries is well known, and it was used to derive an equation that relates the population size with the required solution quality and several domain-dependent parameters.

The accuracy of the model was verified with experiments using test problems that ranged from the very simple to the moderately hard. The results confirmed that the model is accurate, and that its predictions scale well with the difficulty of the domain. In addition, the basic model was extended to consider explicit noise in the fitness evaluation and different selection schemes.

A correctly-sized population is the first step toward competent and efficient genetic algorithms. The next chapter describes how to make single-population GAs faster by using multiple processors to evaluate the fitness of the population in parallel. Subsequent chapters extend the gambler's ruin model to parallel GAs with multiple populations.

Chapter 3

MASTER-SLAVE PARALLEL GENETIC ALGORITHMS

Probably the easiest way to implement GAs on parallel computers is to distribute the evaluation of fitness among several slave processors while one master executes the GA operations (selection, crossover, and mutation). This chapter examines master-slave parallel GAs. These algorithms are important for several reasons: (1) they explore the search space in exactly the same manner as serial GAs, and therefore the existing design guidelines for simple GAs are directly applicable; (2) they are very easy to implement, which makes them popular with practitioners; and (3) in many cases master-slave GAs result in significant improvements in performance. However, there has been little analysis to study the benefits that master-slave parallel GAs offer.

This chapter is focused on a very simple synchronous master-slave GA. Although more efficient implementations are possible, the objective is to give a simple lower bound on the potential benefits that should be expected of parallel GAs in general.

The execution time of master-slave GAs has two basic components: the time used in computations and the time used to communicate information among processors. The computation time is largely determined by the size of the population, so one may be tempted to reduce the population to make the GA faster. However, as the previous chapter discussed, the population size cannot be reduced arbitrarily without suffering a significant decrease in solution quality.

Communication occurs every generation when the master sends individuals to the slaves, and when the slaves return the fitness evaluations to the master. The critical observation made in this chapter is that, as more slaves are used, there is a tradeoff between increasing communications and decreasing the time that each slave uses to evaluate individuals. This tradeoff is used to find the number of slaves that minimize the execution time of the master-slave GA.

The chapter begins with a review of some examples of previous work on master-slave parallel GAs. Section 2 estimates the execution time and shows how to minimize it. Section 3 shows experiments with functions of varying computational requirements that validate the accuracy of the theory, and shows how to calibrate the models to particular hardware and problem domains. Section 4 describes asynchronous algorithms where the master does not wait for the slower slaves before proceeding. Section 5 discusses a variation of the simple master-slave algorithm in which the population is distributed between several processors, but the panmictic property is maintained. This algorithm is important because it similar to a bounding case of multi-deme algorithms that are treated later in the book. Finally, the chapter ends with a brief summary.

1   BACKGROUND

There are many examples of master-slave GAs in the literature. Most of the publications available are from practitioners who need to find solutions to their applications faster, but there are also a few important theoretical studies.

Bethke (1976) was the first to describe parallel implementations of a conventional GA and of a GA with a generation gap (i.e., an algorithm where only a fraction of the population is replaced every generation, see Section 4). He performed a detailed analysis of the efficiency of the use of the processing capacity and concluded that it may be close to 100% if the fitness evaluations are expensive relative to the GA operations, which is usually the case. However, the analysis ignored the cost of communications.

Another early study of master-slave parallel GAs was made by Grefenstette (1981). He proposed four prototypes for parallel GAs. The first three prototypes were variants of a master-slave scheme, and the fourth was a multiple-deme parallel GA. The first prototype was a synchronous master-slave GA similar to the one examined in Section 2. In the second prototype, the fitness evaluations and the replacement of individuals occurred asynchronously, in a manner similar to the algorithm described in Section 4. The third prototype assumes that the population is stored in a global shared memory, and is also an asynchronous algorithm. In addition, Grefenstette briefly hinted at the possibility of combining multiple populations (the fourth prototype) with any of the three master-slave GAs, to create a hybrid parallel GA. Chapter 8 explores this possibility in more detail.

The early works speculated about the benefits that even simple parallel master-slave GAs would bring to domains with long evaluation times.

However, despite the early promises of great speedups, several practitioners stumbled upon a scalability problem: as more processors were used, the efficiency of the parallel algorithm decreased. In most cases, the cause was the increase of communication costs.

For example, Fogarty and Huang (1991) attempted to evolve a set of rules for a pole balancing application that takes a considerable time to simulate. They used a network of transputers, which are microprocessors designed specifically for parallel computations. A transputer connects directly to only four transputers, and communication between arbitrary nodes is handled by retransmitting messages. This causes an overhead in communications, and in an attempt to minimize it, Fogarty and Huang connected the transputers using different topologies. They concluded that the physical configuration of the network did not make a significant difference in the execution time. Although satisfactory reductions of the execution time were reported, they identified the fast-growing communication overhead as an impediment for further improvements.

Abramson and Abela (1992) implemented a GA on a shared-memory computer (an Encore Multimax with 16 processors) to search for school timetables. They reported limited speedups, and blamed a few sections of serial code on the critical path of the program for the results. Later, Abramson, Mills, and Perkins (1993) added a distributed-memory machine (a Fujitsu AP1000 with 128 processors) to the experiments, changed the application to train timetables, and modified the code. This time, they reported good (and almost identical) speedups for up to 16 processors on the two computers, but the speedups degraded significantly with more processors.

Hauser and Männer (1994) used three different parallel computers on their experiments with master-slave GAs, but they obtained good results only on a NERV multiprocessor (speedup of 5 using 6 processors), which has a very low communications overhead. They explained the poor performance on the other systems they used (a SparcServer and a KSR1) on the inadequate scheduling of computation threads to processors by the system.

In general, master-slave implementations are more efficient as the evaluations become more expensive. For instance, Grefenstette (1995) obtained about 80% efficiency on a complex robot learning task, but only 50% with an easier task. Punch et al. (1993) obtained near-linear speedups on a feature selection and classification problem. Their original serial algorithm took over 14 days to run on a Sparc workstation. From their paper, we can estimate that the function evaluation time was over 1.1 sec, which makes this problem an ideal candidate for master-slave parallelization. Section 3 briefly comments on an even more computationally expensive problem that also shows near-linear speedups.

Besides of the evaluation of fitness, we could also parallelize the search operators. For example, recombination and mutation could be parallelized using the same idea of partitioning the population and distributing the work among multiple processors. However, these operators are so simple that any performance gains would be easily offset by the extra time required to send individuals back and forth. The communications cost also complicates the parallelization of selection, mainly because several forms of selection need information about the entire population, and would require excessive exchanges of information. In any case, selection does not contribute significantly to the execution time of the GA, and any improvements in selection would have a very small effect overall.

Despite these obstacles, Section 5 examines an algorithm with a single population that is distributed to several processors. In this algorithm, selection and crossover are parallelized. Although this algorithm requires more communication and is less efficient than the simple master-slave described in the next section, it is important from a theoretical perspective, because it resembles the multi-deme algorithms that occupy most of the remainder of the book.

Of course, the master-slave method can be used to parallelize other evolutionary algorithms, such as evolution strategies (Bäck, 1994a), evolutionary programming (Hirsh & Young, 1998), and genetic programming (Oussaidène, 1997). The models presented in the next section would be applicable to those algorithms as well as to GAs.

2   SYNCHRONOUS MASTER-SLAVES

Recall from Chapter 1 that master-slave GAs can be synchronous or asynchronous, depending on whether they wait to receive the fitness values for the entire population before proceeding to the next generation. Asynchronous master-slave GAs do not wait for any slow slave processors, and have the potential of being more efficient, but their analysis is more difficult. The analysis of this section is for the potentially slower synchronous master-slaves, so the results can be considered as lower bounds of the possible benefits of parallel GAs.

The analysis of master-slave GAs is divided into two sections. The first examines the execution time during one generation of the algorithm. It identifies the primary tradeoff between computation and communications, and finds the configuration that minimizes the execution time. The second section analyzes the parallel efficiency of the algorithm.

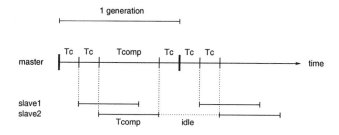

Figure 3.1. One generation in a master-slave parallel GA when the master evaluates a fraction of the population.

2.1   EXECUTION TIME

The calculations presented in this chapter make some simplifying assumptions about the components of the master-slave algorithm. First, the time consumed by selection, crossover, and mutation is ignored, because we may assume that it is much shorter than the time used to evaluate and to communicate individuals. In addition, the analysis considers that the number of individuals assigned to any processor is constant, and that the evaluation time is the same for all individuals.

The analysis of the execution time centers on the master processor. Figure 3.1 depicts the sequence of events in every generation. First, the master sends a fraction of the population to each of the $\mathcal{S}$ slaves, using time T_c to communicate with each. Next, the master evaluates a fraction of the population using time $\frac{nT_f}{\mathcal{P}}$, where T_f is the time required to evaluate one individual, n is the size of the population, and $\mathcal{P} = \mathcal{S} + 1$ is the number of processors used. Implementations where the master stays idle waiting for the results from the slaves are possible, but they would be slower than when the master evaluates a portion of the population.

The slaves start evaluating their portion of the population as soon as they receive it, and return the evaluations to the master as soon as they finish. The last slave and the master finish the evaluation of their shares of individuals at the same time, but there is a delay of time T_c before the master receives the evaluations and can proceed. Considering all the contributions from communications and computations, the elapsed time for one generation of the parallel GA may be estimated as

$$T_p = \mathcal{P}T_c + \frac{nT_f}{\mathcal{P}}. \tag{3.1}$$

As more slaves are used, the computation time decreases as desired, but the communications time increases. This tradeoff entails the existence of an optimal number of processors that minimizes the execution time. To find the optimal, make $\frac{\partial T_p}{\partial \mathcal{P}} = 0$ and solve for $\mathcal{P}$ to obtain

$$\mathcal{P}^* = \sqrt{\frac{nT_f}{T_c}}, \tag{3.2}$$

which can be expressed in a more compact form as $\mathcal{P} = \sqrt{n\gamma}$, where $\gamma = T_f/T_c$. The optimal number of slaves is $\mathcal{S}^* = \mathcal{P}^* - 1$.

Until this point, the calculations have assumed that T_c is constant. More often, the cost of exchanging information between two processors depends on the amount of information, x. Therefore, a better expression for T_c may be $T_c = Bx + L$, where B is the inverse of the bandwidth of the network and L is the latency of communications. The latency is the overhead per message that depends on the operating system, the programming environment, and on the particular hardware. Since each slave receives $n/\mathcal{P}$ individuals, the time required to send them to the slaves is $T_{\text{send}} = B\frac{nl_i}{\mathcal{P}} + L$, and the time to receive the evaluations back is $T_{\text{recv}} = B\frac{nl_f}{\mathcal{P}} + L$, where l_i and l_f are the length of the individuals and of the fitness values, respectively. Estimating the elapsed time per generation as $T_p = \mathcal{S}T_{\text{send}} + T_{\text{recv}} + \frac{nT_f}{\mathcal{P}}$ and optimizing as before, the optimal number of processors becomes

$$\mathcal{P}^* = \sqrt{\frac{n(T_f + B(l_f - l_i))}{L}}, \tag{3.3}$$

which in most cases is not very different from the value given by Equation 3.2, because B is a small number that becomes even smaller as networks get faster. In many cases, the dominant factor in the communications time is the latency, which is constant. Therefore, Equation 3.2 is a good estimator of the optimal number of slaves and can be used confidently to design optimal master-slave GAs.

2.2   SPEEDUPS AND THE BOUND OF ACCEPTABLE PARALLELISM

An important concern when implementing master-slave parallel GAs is that the frequent communications may offset any gains in computation time. The time that a simple GA uses in one generation is $T_s = nT_f$, and to ensure that the parallel implementation is faster than a simple GA the following relationship must hold:

$$\frac{T_s}{T_p} = \frac{nT_f}{\frac{nT_f}{\mathcal{P}} + \mathcal{P}T_c} = \frac{n\gamma}{\frac{n\gamma}{\mathcal{P}} + \mathcal{P}} > 1. \tag{3.4}$$

This ratio is the parallel speedup of the master-slave parallel GA. Solving for γ results in the following necessary condition for better performance in the parallel case:

$$\gamma > \frac{\mathcal{P}^2}{n(\mathcal{P} - 1)}. \tag{3.5}$$

Substituting the minimum number of processors that may be used in parallel ($\mathcal{P} = 2$) into the equation above results in a very compact condition:

$$\gamma > \frac{4}{n}. \tag{3.6}$$

This condition is easy to verify by measuring T_f and T_c on the particular computer that might be used to implement the parallel GA.

The inequality above formalizes the intuitive notion that master-slave GAs do not benefit problems with very short evaluation times. The frequent communications could offset the reduction in the time required to evaluate the population. However, in most problems of interest, the function evaluation time is much greater than the time of communications, $T_f \gg T_c$ ($\gamma \gg 1$), and the population size required to reach an acceptable solution is very large. Therefore, near-linear speedups are possible in many practical problems.

Figure 3.2 shows the theoretical speedups of a master-slave GA varying the value of γ. As γ increases, the range where the speedup is almost linear is wider, and more processors may be used effectively to reduce the execution time. The example considers a master-slave GA with a population of $n = 1000$ individuals, and the speedups are plotted for $\gamma = 1, 10, 100$. In practical problems, the values of γ and n may be higher than those used in the example. The ideal speedup is also plotted as a reference.

Another concern about implementing parallel algorithms is to keep the processor utilization high. After all, an algorithm that does not utilize the processing power in the most efficient way might not be the fastest parallel algorithm. However, note that an algorithm that utilizes the processors at their maximal capacity is not necessarily the fastest algorithm either (because it may be performing unnecessary computations). In any case, the efficiency of a parallel program is a convenient measure that may facilitate further analysis, and may serve to discriminate against algorithms that waste too many resources.

Formally, the parallel efficiency is defined as the ratio of the speedup divided by the number of processors:

$$E_p = \frac{T_s}{T_p \mathcal{P}}. \tag{3.7}$$

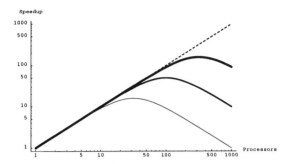

Figure 3.2. Theoretical speedups of a master-slave GA varying the value of γ. The thinest line corresponds to $\gamma = 1$, the intermediate to $\gamma = 10$, and the thickest to $\gamma = 100$. The dotted line is the ideal (linear) speedup.

In an ideal situation, the efficiency would always be one and the parallel speedup would be equal to the number of processors used. In reality, the cost of communications prevents this from happening, and the efficiency measures the deviation from the ideal situation. For example, an efficiency of 0.8 means that the algorithm is performing at 80% of its ideal potential. Later in this section we shall see that there is no sense in using an algorithm with an efficiency of less than 0.5.

Figure 3.3 shows an example that illustrates how the efficiency drops as more processors are used. The example considers a population of 1000 individuals and $\gamma = 10$. The ideal speedup and the expected speedups (as predicted by Equation 3.4) are also displayed. In this example, the relatively high costs of communications cause the efficiency to decrease fast; but in situations with a higher γ, the efficiency would remain close to one for a wider range of processors, and the speedup would be near-linear.

We may calculate the critical number of processors that maintain a desired efficiency $\widehat{E_p}$ by making Equation 3.7 equal to $\widehat{E_p}$ and solving for $\mathcal{P}$:

$$\mathcal{P}_c = \sqrt{\frac{1 - \widehat{E_p}}{\widehat{E_p}}} \sqrt{\frac{nT_f}{T_c}}, \tag{3.8}$$

which is a fraction of the optimal number of processors $\mathcal{P}^*$.

An interesting application of this equation is to calculate the critical number of processors where the efficiency equals $1 - \frac{1}{\mathcal{P}}$. At this point, the deviation from the ideal efficiency represents losing one processor to the communications overhead. To determine this critical number of processors, which we denote as $\mathcal{P}_l$, we substitute $\widehat{E_p} = 1 - \frac{1}{\mathcal{P}_l}$ into

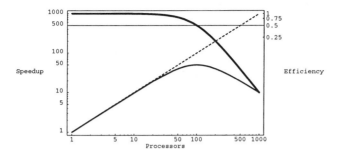

Figure 3.3. The algorithmic efficiency (bold line) decreases as more slaves are used. The figure also shows the ideal speedup (dotted line) and the speedup with communications.

Equation 3.8. Simplifying terms yields

$$\mathcal{P}_l^3 + \mathcal{P}_l^2 = \frac{nT_f}{T_c} = (\mathcal{P}^*)^2. \tag{3.9}$$

Asymptotically, we may ignore the $\mathcal{P}_l^2$ term and solve for $\mathcal{P}_l$ to obtain

$$\mathcal{P}_l = (\mathcal{P}^*)^{2/3} = (\gamma n)^{1/3}. \tag{3.10}$$

Besides of its benefit as a guide to maintain a high level of processor utilization, the calculation of the critical number of processors (Equation 3.8) permits to calculate the maximum speedup of master-slave GAs in a simple way. First, realize that $\mathcal{P}_c = \mathcal{P}^*$ only when $\widehat{E_p}$ is $1/2$ (see Figure 3.3). If the efficiency of the algorithm is $1/2$ when the optimal number of processors is used, then using the definition of efficiency,

$$E_p = \frac{1}{2} = \frac{S_p}{\mathcal{P}^*}, \tag{3.11}$$

and solving for S_p, gives the maximum speedup possible as

$$S_p^* = \frac{1}{2}\mathcal{P}^*. \tag{3.12}$$

This simple calculation represents a practical lower bound on the potential speedups of parallel GAs. It is a bound in the sense that other parallel GAs *should* do no worse than the simplest master-slave. While it is possible that other parallel GAs cannot deliver higher speedups, those algorithms should be discarded.

However, there is plenty of room for improvement. At their optimal configuration, master-slave GAs have an efficiency of 50%: half of the time the processors are idle or are communicating with their peers. Surely, there must be other parallel GAs that can use the available processing power in more efficient ways and yield solutions of the same quality in less time. Section 4 and the following chapters explore some of those algorithms in detail. The next section presents experimental results that validate the accuracy of the analysis of master-slaves.

3   EXPERIMENTS

This section describes experiments with a particular master-slave implementation on a network of IBM RS/6000 workstations. The workstations are connected by a 10 Mbits/sec Ethernet and all communications are implemented using PVM 3.3. This is a rather slow communications environment, and Equation 3.6 indicates that no performance improvements are expected with simple test functions. For this reason, the first three sets of experiments use an artificial function that can be altered easily to change its evaluation time (T_f). The fourth set of experiments uses a complex neural network application that takes a very long time to evaluate.

The test problem for the first three sets of experiments is a dummy function that consists in a simple loop with a single addition that can be repeated an arbitrary number of times. The length of the individuals was set to 80 bytes and the population size to 120 individuals. The master-slave GA was executed for 10 generations, and the results reported are the average of 30 runs. We determined empirically that the latency of communications on our system was approximately $T_c = 19$ milliseconds.

The results of the experiments are summarized in Figure 3.4. The figure shows the elapsed time per generation of the master-slave GA varying the number of slaves from 1 to 9 (only ten computers were available for this experiment). For the first experiment, the evaluation time of the test function was set to 2 milliseconds. With the results of the previous section, we can calculate the optimal number of slaves as $\mathcal{S}^* = \sqrt{\frac{nT_f}{T_c}} - 1 = \sqrt{\frac{120(2)}{19}} - 1 = 2.55$. In the second experiment, the evaluation time of the test function was doubled to 4 ms, and the model predicts that the optimal number of slaves is $\mathcal{S}^* = 4.02$. The evaluation time was doubled again for the third experiment to $T_f = 8$ ms, and for this case $\mathcal{S}^* = 6.1$.

The last experiment uses a more complex evaluation function. It is an application where the GA searched for the weights of the connections of a neural network with 13 inputs, 30 units in the hidden layer, and 5 output units. The objective was to classify a set of 738 vectors that represent sleep patterns into 5 classes. The evaluation function decoded

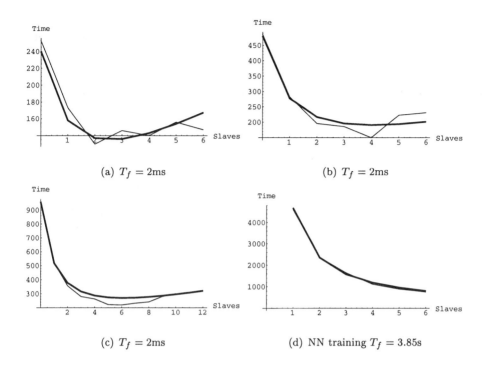

Figure 3.4. Elapsed time (ms) per generation on a master-slave GA varying the number of slaves. The thick lines are the theoretical predictions (Eq. 3.1, and the thin lines are the experimental results.

the weights from a string of 5150 bytes, tested the network with each of the patterns, and calculated the percentage of the classifications made correctly. The population size was set to 120 individuals and on our computers each evaluation takes 3.85 seconds, which makes this problem an ideal candidate for the master-slave method. As we can see in Figure 3.4d, the elapsed time decreased linearly with the number of slaves. In fact, the communications overhead is so small that for this problem $\mathcal{S}^* = 151$ processors.

4   ASYNCHRONOUS MASTER-SLAVES

Section 2 showed that the efficiency of a parallel master-slave algorithm is 50% at its optimal configuration. Basically, half of the time the processors are idle, waiting for the master to assign them work. The master, however, cannot assign work to the slaves sooner because it must wait for *all* the slaves to finish the fitness evaluations before selecting the parents to the next generation. This generational synchronization is necessary to ensure that the master-slave produces exactly the same results as a simple serial GA, but it is easy to avoid if we are willing to accept a different behavior of the algorithm.

In asynchronous master-slave GAs, the master generates individuals and sends them to the slaves to be evaluated. As soon as a slave finishes its share of the evaluations, the master inserts the evaluated individual(s) into the population. Then, the master generates new individuals, and sends them to any available slaves. Asynchronous master-slaves have the potential to be more efficient than the synchronous algorithm (e.g., Zeigler and Kim (1993), Stanley and Mudge (1995)), especially if the evaluation times are not constant for all individuals, but they introduce additional parameters. In particular, there are several options about how many individuals are generated at a time, and about how they are incorporated into the population.

Asynchronous master-slaves resemble GAs with a generation gap, because there is no clear separation between generations. De Jong (1975) introduced the generation gap, $G \in [\frac{1}{n}, 1]$, as a parameter that determines the fraction of the population that the GA replaces every generation. The simple GA replaces the entire population, so $G = 1$, and at the other extreme, the so-called "steady-state" GAs create one individual per iteration, so $G = \frac{1}{n}$.

The differences between generational GAs and GAs with a generation gap arise from the way in which they insert new individuals into the population, which must be determined for the master-slave GAs as well. Whitley (1989) proposed a steady-state GA called GENITOR that replaces the worst individual in the population with the newly-created individual. Whitley recognized that GENITOR has a higher selection pressure than the traditional GA, and that the algorithm requires larger populations to succeed, which is consistent with the results in Chapter 2. On the other hand, Syswerda (1991) showed that the dynamics of the GA are unaffected when individuals are replaced randomly. Others have studied the effect of the replacement method on the takeover time (a measure of selection pressure) using Markov chains (Chakraborty et al., 1996; Smith & Vavak, 1999; Rudolph, 2000b). These studies confirmed Whitley's and Syswerda's earlier observations. More recently, Cantú-Paz (2000c) quantified the increase of the selection intensity as a function of G, and Rogers and Prügel-Bennett (1999) described the dynamics of the distribution of fitness.

Asynchronous master-slaves have the same choices as GAs with generation gaps: the newly-evaluated individuals can be inserted randomly, replace the worst, or compete against other individuals to gain a spot in the population. If the insertion is based on the new individual's fitness, the selection pressure will increase, and the existing theory (see Chapter 2) suggests that the algorithm would need larger populations to obtain the same solution quality as the algorithm with lower pressure.

The asynchronous parallelism may have other effects on the algorithm besides increasing the selection pressure. The most notable is that individuals may return from the slaves in a different order in which they were created, because some slaves will finish their evaluations faster than others. We could avoid this issue if we wait for the slower processors and insert the individuals in order, but that would not be as efficient. Davison and Rasheed (1999) identified this problem and systematically studied the effect of allowing random returns while varying the number of slaves in the experiments. Their steady-state algorithm replaced a low-fit individual that is similar to the new one. Experimenting with several standard design benchmarks and a supersonic aircraft design problem, they concluded that the effect of accepting individuals in random order was very small, even when the number of slaves was close to the population size.

Asynchronous master-slave GAs are only slightly more difficult to implement than the synchronous, and the gains in performance may easily offset the extra cost of development. However, we will ignore them in the remainder, as they are more difficult to analyze.

5   A DISTRIBUTED PANMICTIC POPULATION

An alternative to store the entire population in one master node is to distribute the population to several processors. If we want the distributed population to behave as a single panmictic unit, the algorithm must be modified: selection and crossover should consider the entire population. The algorithm with a distributed panmictic population is important because it resembles a bounding case of multi-deme parallel GAs, and therefore the calculations presented below shed some light on the expected performance of this class of algorithms. The form of the execution time of the algorithm with a distributed population is very similar to the time of a simple master-slave algorithm, so the calculations in this section are very similar to those in Section 2.

Let n denote the population size required to reach the desired quality in a particular problem. The population is partitioned into equally-sized parts and distributed to $\mathcal{P}$ processors. In every generation, all the nodes perform the four basic GA tasks on their fraction of the population: fitness evaluation, selection, crossover, and mutation. The evaluation of fitness and mutation are not an issue because they can be performed on each fraction of the population independently. However, to ensure that the distributed population behaves as a panmictic one, the selection and crossover operations must be modified. We begin the presentation of the algorithm with the parallel implementation of crossover, because ensuring that every individual is considered exactly once is straightforward.

In a sequential GA, each selected individual forms part of exactly one mating pair per generation. The pairs are formed randomly, and any two individuals in the population may be chosen to mate. To maintain this property in the parallel GA, each of the $\mathcal{P}$ processors randomly divides its fraction of the population into $\mathcal{P}$ equally-sized parts and sends each part to a different processor. These communications take time $T_x = (\mathcal{P} - 1)T_c$, where T_c is the average time used to communicate with one processor. The processors incorporate the incoming individuals into their fractions of the population by replacing the individuals sent to a particular deme with the individuals received from it. Then, each processor randomly chooses pairs of mates, and proceeds to exchange material between them. There are, of course, other ways to preserve the panmictic property in a distributed population (e.g., Braud and Vrain (1999)), but the calculations would be similar.

The required modifications to selection are specific to the selection method used (there is a description of selection methods in Chapter 7). For example, proportional selection requires the average of the fitness of the population, so a global communication would be required to pass this information to all the processors. After calculating the probabilities of survival and performing selection, it is likely that some processors have more individuals than others, and some extra communication would be needed to redistribute the individuals evenly among the processors. Other selection methods are based on the rank of the individuals, so the population must be sorted before selecting the parents. To illustrate the modifications to selection, we consider only tournament selection, but the calculations could be extended to the other types of selection. Recall that tournament selection without replacement works by choosing non-overlapping random sets of s individuals from the population, and then selecting the best individual from each set to serve as a parent for the next generation. There are n/s such sets, and each tournament produces one winner; therefore, to generate all the parents for the next generation, it is necessary to repeat this procedure s times. Any individual in the population may participate in any given tournament, and the key idea in the parallel algorithm is to maintain this property.

The first step in the parallel selection consists on each processor randomly dividing its fraction of the population into $\mathcal{P}$ equally-sized parts, and sending a different part to every other processor. These communications take time $(\mathcal{P} - 1)T_c$. The processors receive and incorporate the individuals into their fraction of the population. Then, each processor picks random non-overlapping sets of s individuals to compete in tournaments. Note that the individuals who participate in a given tournament may have been received from any processor, or may have been already present in the processor. In any case, all the individuals in the population have the same chance to participate in a given tournament, just as they do in the serial case. To select all the parents for the next generation, the process has to be repeated s times, and therefore the total communication time is $T_s = s(\mathcal{P} - 1)T_c$.

The computation time per node is simply $\frac{nT_f}{\mathcal{P}}$. Communications are used during both selection (T_s) and crossover (T_x). The general form of the time used in communications during selection is $T_s = \kappa_s(\mathcal{P} - 1)T_c$, where κ_s is a constant that depends on the selection method. In the case of tournament selection κ_s equals the size of the tournament, s. The communication time used during crossover is $T_x = (\mathcal{P} - 1)T_c$, so we may write the total time used in communications as $(\kappa_s+1)(\mathcal{P}-1)T_c$. To simplify the calculations we define $\kappa = \kappa_s + 1$. Adding computation and communications times we obtain the total execution time per generation:

$$T_p = \frac{nT_f}{\mathcal{P}} + \kappa(\mathcal{P} - 1)T_c. \qquad (3.13)$$

As before, when more processors are used there is a tradeoff between decreasing computations and increasing communications. Solving $\frac{\partial T_p}{\partial \mathcal{P}} = 0$ for $\mathcal{P}$ we obtain the optimal number of processors that minimize the execution time:

$$\mathcal{P}^* = \sqrt{\frac{nT_f}{\kappa T_c}}. \qquad (3.14)$$

In the case of a traditional master-slave algorithm there is only one communications event per generation ($\kappa = 1$), and the result above agrees with the calculations in Section 2.

Although there are multiple communications per generation, in many practical situations the function evaluation time is much longer than the time of communications, $T_f \gg T_c$, and the population is considerably large. Under these conditions, the optimal number of processors can be quite large, and we can expect near-linear speedups for a wide range of processors.

6   SUMMARY

Master-slave parallel GAs are easy to implement, often yield considerable improvements in performance, and all the theory available for simple GAs can be used to choose adequate values for the search parameters. The analysis of this chapter showed that, for many applications, the reduction in computation time is sufficient to overcome the cost of communications. The calculations presented here should be useful to design fast master-slave GAs that utilize the computing resources in the best possible way.

The chapter discussed the similarities between asynchronous master-slave GAs and GAs with a generation gap. The chapter also presented a GA with a single distributed population. This algorithm is less efficient than the simple master-slave, but it is important because it resembles a GA with multiple communicating populations. The analysis of this algorithm reveals that the optimal number of processors is of the same order as the master-slave.

The main contribution of this chapter was to present a lower bound on the performance gains that are acceptable in any parallel GAs. More sophisticated single-population GAs or multi-population parallel GAs should do better than the simple case examined here or they should be abandoned. The calculations are simple and they are easy to calibrate to consider the hardware and the particular problem.

Chapter 4

BOUNDING CASES OF GENETIC ALGORITHMS WITH MULTIPLE DEMES

The first part of the book discussed GAs with a single population. Now we shift our attention to parallel GAs with multiple populations, which are the most popular type. This class of parallel GAs are also called "coarse-grained" or "distributed" GAs, because the communication to computation ratio is low, and they are often implemented on distributed-memory computers. They are also known as "island model" GAs because they resemble a model that is used to describe natural populations that are relatively isolated from each other, as in islands. Both in the island model and in the GAs, individuals may migrate occasionally to any other population.

The design of multiple-deme parallel GAs involves difficult and related choices. The main issues are to determine (1) the size and the number of demes, (2) the topology that interconnects the demes, (3) the migration rate that controls how many individuals migrate, (4) the frequency of migration that determines how often migrations occur, and (5) the migration policy that determines which individuals migrate and which are replaced in the receiving deme. These choices are complicated, and most of this book is dedicated to examine them: this chapter begins the study of multi-deme GAs that will end in Chapter 7.

Many studies of parallel GAs are empirical investigations that concentrate on the choices of topologies and migration rates and treat the population-sizing issue as a secondary problem. However, since the population size largely determines the quality of the solution (Goldberg et al., 1992; Harik et al., 1997) and the duration of the run (Goldberg & Deb, 1991), it is only natural that our study of multiple-deme parallel GAs begins by addressing this issue.

However, we cannot ignore the importance of topologies and migration rates, because they have unknown effects on the algorithm's efficiency and on the quality of the solutions. We can gain some insight into the effects of these parameters by studying parallel GAs that use the minimum and maximum bounding values. Therefore, in this chapter we consider two bounding cases of parallel GAs. The first bound is a set of simple GAs running in parallel with no interactions between them. The model for this completely isolated case is a straightforward extension of the gambler's ruin model introduced in Chapter 2. In the second bounding case, each deme exchanges individuals with all the others, and the migration rate is set to a maximum value.

Although it is more likely that users set the connectivity and the migration rate to intermediate values, the bounding cases serve as indicators of the performance of parallel GAs. Once the simplifications and assumptions used in this chapter are shown to be viable, the models will be specialized later.

The results of this chapter show that the speedup is not very significant when the demes are isolated, but there is a substantial improvement in performance when the demes communicate. Moreover, in the fully-connected case, there is a deme count and deme size that together minimize the parallel speedup.

The next section is a brief review of related work on multi-deme parallel GAs. Section 2 briefly discusses parallel speedups and the way that performance will be measured in this study. Section 3 extends the gambler's ruin model to the isolated case, and Section 4 considers fully connected demes. The chapter ends with a brief summary in Section 5.

1   BACKGROUND

Despite the difficulties in their design, multi-deme parallel GAs have been very popular, and the literature contains many reports of successful implementations. This section gives a short historical account of some of the relevant work in this area. Further examples can be found elsewhere (Cantú-Paz, 1998a).

Bossert (1967) was probably the first to propose an evolutionary algorithm with multiple populations to improve the quality of the solutions in an optimization problem. Bossert's populations compete for survival with each other, in a manner analogous to Wright's (1932) demes (see Chapter 1). Bossert proposed two mechanisms to promote the diversity necessary to explore the search space. The first was to eliminate the worst population at random intervals, and create new populations arbitrarily after the beginning of the experiment. The second mechanism was to introduce diversity either by migration or by changing the fitness measure over time.[1]

Grefenstette (1981) described an early parallel GA with multiple populations. In his algorithm, the best individuals from each deme are broadcast every generation to all the others. Grefenstette recognized the complexity of coarse-grained parallel GAs, and raised several "interesting questions" about the frequency of migration, the destination of the migrants (topology), and the effect of migration on preventing premature convergence to suboptimal solutions. Those are the questions that will occupy us for most of the remainder of this book.

Grosso (1985) was the first to observe some of the phenomena that continue to appear in the literature. For instance, he observed that the rate of fitness improvement was faster in a population divided into demes than in a single panmictic population (which is consistent with the shifting balance theory). But if the demes remained isolated for the entire experiment, the final solution's quality was lower than that reached by a single panmictic population of equivalent size. Grosso experimented with a wide range of migration rates, and observed that with intermediate settings the partitioned and the panmictic populations reached solutions with the same quality. In his first experiments, migrations occurred every generation, and the migrants and their destinations were selected randomly. Grosso also tried a "delayed" migration scheme in which communications began only after the demes were near convergence. Then, the demes exchanged individuals with a high migration rate. The delayed scheme reduced the cost of communications and resulted in solutions of the same quality as those obtained with frequent migrations. Later, this chapter presents an analysis of the solution quality that can be reached by an algorithm with a similar migration scheme.

Braun (1990) used a similar idea to Grosso's delayed migration and presented an algorithm where migration occurred after the demes converged completely (he used the term "degenerate"). The explicit purpose of migration was to restore diversity into the demes to prevent them to converge prematurely to a inferior solution. Later, Munetomo, Takai, and Sato (1993) adopted a similar strategy where migration was triggered when the population's diversity fell below a certain level. In this case, the topology of communications was not fixed: migrants were sent

---

[1]Interestingly, Bossert recognized that the dynamic environments would introduce additional problems if the changes are drastic or occur frequently. Others have observed that migration (Grefenstette, 1992) and the shifting balance model can be effective to improve the performance of GAs in dynamic environments (Oppacher & Wineberg, 1999).

to populations with low diversity. Using dynamic topologies is an interesting idea that has been explored and extended in multiple ways (e.g., (Norman, 1989; Pettey & Leuze, 1989; Nowostawski & Poli, 1999)).

Tanese initiated the systematic study of migration and its effects on the efficiency and quality of parallel GAs (Tanese, 1987; 1989a; 1989b). Her experimental method consisted in dividing a fixed number of individuals into equally-sized demes, and to vary the migration rates and the migration intervals.

Tanese's experiments showed that medium migration rates are necessary to find solutions of the same quality as with a serial GA. A migration rate that was too low or too high resulted in lesser solutions. Like Grosso, Tanese examined completely isolated demes and found that the solutions were generally inferior to those found by a serial GA or by the parallel GA with migration. In terms of the efficiency of the parallel algorithm, she found that "near-linear" speedups can be obtained when migration is infrequent and the migration rate is low.

Implicit in Tanese's experimental method is the assumption that several small populations can be compared fairly against one aggregate population. Keeping the total number of individuals constant seems to be adequate for a fair experimental design, but since the quality and cost depend non-linearly on the deme size, neither the cost or the quality were held constant in the experiments. Unfortunately, others also treat the questions of efficiency and quality separately, and—not surprisingly—reports of linear, quasi-linear, or super-linear speedups appear constantly in the literature. These controversial claims will be considered further in Chapter 7.

In any case, Tanese's groundbreaking study identified many of the important issues for the correct design of parallel GAs: the choice of one or many populations, the frequency of migrations, and the migration rate. In addition, she studied how the migration parameters affect the loss of allele diversity. To prevent the premature loss of useful solutions, she proposed to set the GA parameters differently in each population, causing some populations to converge slower than others. For example, the populations may use different crossover types or crossover probabilities and different selection methods. The idea is that diversity is preserved longer in the populations that converge slowly, and migration would reintroduce diversity into the populations that were set to converge quickly.

Others have adopted successfully Tanese's idea of using different parameters in each population to try to balance exploration and exploitation (e.g., (Lin et al., 1994; Adamidis & Petridis, 1996; Herrera & Lozano, 2000)). This heterogeneous approach seems to produce good results and is important to consider, especially when there is no a priori information that can guide the choice of selection and recombination (using, for instance, the results of Goldberg, Deb, and Thierens (1993)). A notable heterogeneous algorithm is the injection-island system of Lin et al. (1994) that uses different representations in each deme. The representations vary in their resolution, and the populations are arranged in a hierarchical topology where migration only occurs from low to high-resolution populations. The algorithm has been tested successfully in several design applications (Punch et al., 1995; Goodman et al., 1997).

The scalability of parallel GAs to large problem sizes has been demonstrated experimentally in multiple occasions. For instance, Mühlenbein et al. (1991) solved a highly multimodal problem (the Rastrigin function) with 400 variables; Levine (1994) found the optimal solutions of set partitioning problems with a few thousand integer variables, and found good solutions to problems with 36,699 and 43,749 variables.

An early attempt to provide a theoretical foundation to the performance of parallel GAs was a derivation of the schema theorem that considered that randomly-selected individuals are broadcast every generation (Pettey & Leuze, 1989). The calculations showed that the expected number of trials allocated to schemata are consistent with the original schema theorem for simple GAs.

A very important question is to determine if, and under what conditions, a parallel GA can find a better solution than a serial GA. Starkweather, Whitley, and Mathias (1991) observed that relatively isolated demes are likely to evolve in different directions. It is possible that individuals in separate demes match different portions of the global solution, and, after the individuals are brought together by migration, they can recombine to form better solutions. Starkweather et al. speculated that this is more likely to happen if the objective function is separable (i.e., combining partial solutions yields a better individual), and therefore parallel GAs may have an advantage in this case. However, if the recombination of partial solutions results in individuals with lower fitness (perhaps because the function is not separable), then the serial GA might be preferable. These results were confirmed later by Whitley et al. (1999) using a Markov chain model.

Of course, the island model can be used with other evolutionary algorithms, not just GAs. For example, Rudolph (1991) experimented with distributed evolution strategies, and he noticed that they may have an advantage in separable functions, which is consistent with Starkweather et al.'s observations in GAs. Another evolutionary algorithm that has been successfully parallelized with the island model is genetic programming (GP), which usually requires very large populations. Koza and

Andre (1995) described an early implementation on a transputer network, and Koza et al. (1999) described more recent implementations on Beowulf-style clusters with up to 1000 Pentium processors that reach human-competitive results in some problems. Oussaidène (1997) described a parallel GP system for financial applications, and made a very detailed analysis of the system's efficiency and scalability.

There have also been efforts to parallelize messy GAs (Goldberg et al., 1989). Messy GAs have two phases: the primordial phase that uses a partial enumeration to create the initial population, and the juxtapositional phase that mixes the partial solutions found in the primordial phase. The primordial phase dominates the execution time, and Merkle and Lamont (1993) tried several data distribution strategies to speed up this phase, extending previous work by Dymek (1992). Their results showed substantial gains in the execution time of the algorithm and no significant differences in the quality of the solutions. Merkle et al. (1998) parallelized a *fast* messy GA (Goldberg et al., 1993) to search for optimal conformations of molecules.

This chapter uses an approach that differs from many investigations of parallel GAs: it acknowledges that the solution quality and algorithmic efficiency are strongly related, and the analysis considers them simultaneously. This is the main reason why some of the results of this chapter may disagree with the results of others.

2   PARALLEL SPEEDUPS

The conventional definition of the parallel speedup of an algorithm is the ratio of the execution time of the best serial algorithm, T_s, and the execution time of the parallel program, T_p (Almasi & Gottlieb, 1994). In our case, we consider that the best serial algorithm is a GA with a population just large enough to reach the desired quality and that uses the same operators as the parallel GA. Excessively large populations in the serial GA result in inflated speedups, and therefore should be avoided in comparisons. We must recognize that parallel GAs with multiple demes are different algorithms from simple GAs with one population, so we will be talking about the relative speedup between two different algorithms, and not about the speedup between the serial and parallel versions of the same algorithm, as in the master-slave case.

In the GA community, there has been some controversy about parallel speedups in GAs with multiple demes. The primary disagreement arises from the frequent claims of superlinear speedups (i.e., the execution time of the parallel GA is reduced by a factor greater than the number of processors used).

In general, to make a fair comparison between any serial and parallel programs the two must give exactly the same result; and in the case of stochastic algorithms like GAs, a fair comparison should be based on the *expected* quality of convergence. Some claims of superlinear speedups are suspicious because serial and parallel GAs were compared without explicitly considering the quality of the solutions. Sometimes an experimental design that seems fair because it holds constant one of the important variables (like the total number of individuals) is inadequate because the solution quality is not guaranteed to remain constant. The analysis in this chapter avoids this problem, and makes fair comparisons of serial and parallel GAs that reach *on average* a solution of the same quality. The claims of superlinear speedups are addressed further in Chapter 7.

Besides the superlinear speedups, another source of controversy is that often it is not clear how performance is measured. Sometimes it is convenient to use the number of function evaluations, because different algorithms may be compared regardless of their implementation details. More often, the performance is measured by recording the wall-clock time, so all the components of the execution time—including communications—are accounted. The wall-clock time is a fair measure, and it is the one used in this study.

3 ISOLATED DEMES

The first bounding case of parallel GAs considers that the demes evolve in complete isolation. Without communication, the migration rate is zero, and this is clearly a lower bound. Also, no connections between the demes represent a lower bound in the connectivity of the topology.

3.1 EXPECTED QUALITY AND DEME SIZE

The first step in the analysis is to determine the target quality, $\hat{P}$, required in each deme. We may be conservative and simply use the required solution's quality, $\hat{Q}$, but in a setup with multiple demes, the chance that at least one of them succeeds increases as more demes are used. Therefore, the per-deme target quality can be relaxed, and the following paragraphs show how to compute that relaxation.[2]

The quality of the solution is measured as the number of partitions that converge correctly, Q. Recall from Chapter 2 that the probability that one partition converges correctly is given by the gambler's ruin

---

[2]Cantú-Paz and Goldberg (1997a) used a different (but mathematically equivalent) method to reach the same result of this section.

model, P_{bb}. Under the assumption that the m partitions are independent from each other, the quality has a binomial distribution with parameters m and P_{bb}. The expected solution quality is $E(Q) = mP_{bb}$, but, of course, some demes will reach better solutions than others. In a system with r demes, we may write the qualities of the solutions of the demes in ascending order as

$$Q_{1:r} \leq Q_{2:r} \leq \cdots \leq Q_{r:r}.$$

These are the *order statistics* of the solution quality of the r demes. $Q_{1:r}$ denotes the quality of the worst solution found by the r demes, and $Q_{r:r}$ denotes the quality of the best solution found. We are interested in designing the parallel GA so that the expected value of $Q_{r:r}$ be equal to the desired quality $\hat{Q}$. Unfortunately, there is no closed-form expression for the mean values of the maximal order statistics of samples greater then five, but these values have been tabulated extensively for the standard normal distribution (see Table 4.1, taken from (Harter, 1970)). To take advantage of this, the binomial distribution of the quality may be approximated with a Gaussian distribution, and the number of correct partitions can be normalized as $Z_{i:r} = \frac{Q_{i:r} - mP_{bb}}{\sqrt{mP_{bb}(1 - P_{bb})}}$. The expected quality of the best deme is $E(Z_{r:r}) = \mu_{r:r}$, where $\mu_{r:r}$ denotes the mean of the highest-order statistic of a standard Gaussian distribution. The expected value of $Q_{r:r}$ is

$$\hat{Q} = E(Q_{r:r}) = mP_{bb} + \mu_{r:r}\sqrt{mP_{bb}(1 - P_{bb})}. \tag{4.1}$$

Since the expected quality of the solution is mP_{bb}, the benefit of using multiple isolated demes is given by the second term of the equation above. Unfortunately, $\mu_{r:r}$ grows very slowly as r increases, and therefore the quality in the best deme is only slightly better than the quality reached by a single deme. Actually, we can easily bound $E(Q_{r:r})$ by realizing that $P_{bb}(1 - P_{bb})$ is maximal when $P_{bb} = 0.5$, so

$$\hat{Q} = E(Q_{r:r}) \leq mP_{bb} + \frac{\mu_{r:r}}{2}\sqrt{m}. \tag{4.2}$$

We ignore the inequality and solve this equation for P_{bb} to obtain the required probability of success per deme as

$$\hat{P} = \frac{\hat{Q}}{m} - \frac{\mu_{r:r}}{2\sqrt{m}}. \tag{4.3}$$

This equation clearly shows how the required probability of success per deme is relaxed as more demes are used. It may be approximated asymptotically using $\mu_{r:r} \approx \sqrt{2 \ln r}$ (Beyer, 1993) as

$$\hat{P} = \frac{\hat{Q}}{m} - \frac{\sqrt{\ln r}}{\sqrt{2m}}, \tag{4.4}$$

Table 4.1. Expected values of the highest order statistic $\mu_{r:r}$ of a unit normal distribution for representative values of r.

r	1	2	4	8	16	32	64	128	256
$\mu_{r:r}$	0	0.5642	1.029	1.423	1.766	2.069	2.343	2.594	2.826

which shows that $\hat{P}$ decreases very slowly with respect to r.[3] To find the deme size we use the gambler's ruin problem in a manner similar to Section 3. We must now solve $\hat{P} = P_{bb} = 1 - \left(\frac{q}{p}\right)^{n_d/2^k}$ for n_d, and the result is

$$n_d = \frac{2^k \ln(1 - \hat{P})}{\ln\left(\frac{q}{p}\right)}, \qquad (4.5)$$

which can be approximated in terms of the domain signal and noise as

$$n_d = 2^{k-1} \ln(1 - \hat{P}) \sqrt{\pi m'} \frac{\sigma_{bb}}{d}. \qquad (4.6)$$

This equation is similar to the population size of the simple GA found in Chapter 2. The only difference is that the quality required to succeed now $(\hat{P})$ is slightly smaller than before $(\hat{Q}/m)$. Note that $\hat{P}$ is equal to $\hat{Q}/m$ when $r = 1$.

3.2   SPEEDUPS

The calculations of this section assume that there is one processor for every deme, so the parallel execution time, T_p, is the time used by *one* deme to complete its tasks (computations and communications). As in the calculations of Chapter 3, we assume that the computation time is dominated by the time used to evaluate the objective function, and thus we ignore the time used in the GA operations—selection, crossover, and mutation.

When the demes are isolated, the communication time is null, and only the computation times are necessary to calculate the expected speedup. In every generation, the GA evaluates all its population, using time T_f to evaluate each individual. The number of generations until convergence may be assumed to be a domain-dependent constant, g. Holding the

---

[3]I discovered that $\mu_{r:r}$ can be approximated more accurately as $\mu_{r:r} = \sqrt{\sqrt{2}\ln r}$. However, this does not change the conclusions of this section.

quality constant the speedup for isolated demes is

$$S_p = \frac{gnT_f}{gn_dT_f} = \frac{n}{n_d}. \qquad (4.7)$$

Substituting the population sizes for the serial and isolated parallel GAs (Equations 2.9 and 4.5, respectively) into Equation 4.7 and simplifying terms gives a simple equation for the speedup (Cantú-Paz & Goldberg, 1997b):

$$S_p = \frac{\ln(1 - \frac{\hat{Q}}{m})}{\ln(1 - \hat{P})}. \qquad (4.8)$$

Note that the only problem-dependent parameter in this equation is m, the number of partitions of the problem. Since $\hat{P}$ decreases very slowly with respect to r, the equation above shows that we cannot expect a large speedup from isolated demes. The accuracy of this equation was verified with experiments using the 4-bit and 8-bit deceptive trap functions that were used in Chapter 2 to test the GR model. In the experiments, the isolated demes used the same parameters as the GAs in Chapter 2: pairwise tournament selection, the crossover probability was set to 1.0, and the mutation probability was zero. Two-point and one-point crossover were used for the 4-bit and 8-bit trap, respectively. For each deme count ($r = 1, 2, ..., 16$), the deme size was increased until at least one of the demes found a solution with at least $\frac{\hat{Q}}{m} = 80\%$ of correct BBs. The results shown in this section are the average of 100 independent runs. The theoretical predictions for the parallel speedup along with the experimental results are plotted in Figure 4.1.

The experiments confirm that there is only a modest advantage in using isolated demes. Therefore, it is advisable to avoid this bounding case in practice.

4   FULLY-CONNECTED DEMES

Executing demes in complete isolation is clearly a bound for parallel GAs, as the migration rate is zero, and there are no connections between the demes. This section examines algorithms at the opposite extreme: every deme exchanges individuals with all the others and the migration rate is set to its maximum value.

Another important parameter is the migration frequency. The upper bound of the frequency of migration is to exchange individuals every generation. This bound represents the most intense communication possible: fully-connected demes that communicate every generation with the maximal migration rates. Notice that the algorithm with a distributed

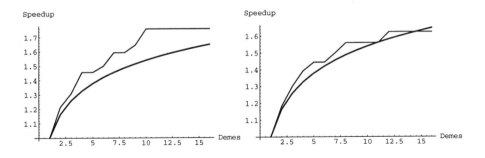

(a) 4-bit trap function with 20 BBs.   (b) 8-bit trap function with 10 BBs.

Figure 4.1.   Predicted and experimental speedups for deceptive trap functions using 1 to 16 isolated demes. The thin line shows the experimental results and the thick line is the theoretical prediction. The quality demanded in both cases was to find 80% of correct BBs.

panmictic population described in Chapter 3 resembles this bounding case. Recall that in that algorithm each processor executes essentially a complete GA (fitness evaluation, selection, crossover, and mutation), and there is an exchange of individuals every generation. The topology of communication is a complete graph, because each processor exchanges individuals with every other during selection and crossover, and the number of individuals exchanged is $n/\mathcal{P}$, which corresponds to the maximal migration rate. Chapter 3 presented how to estimate and minimize the execution time of this algorithm.

However, the distributed population algorithm has *multiple* communications per generation, and this is its major difference with multi-deme GAs, which have *at most one* migration event in a generation. In multi-deme GAs, selection and recombination consider only a subset of the population, and the search may be biased toward some region of the search space. There have been no studies of this bias, but it may be not very strong if migration occurs as often as every generation.

Another difference is that in multi-population algorithms the migrants and the individuals that they replace can be chosen in different ways. In particular, the outgoing migrants can be the best individuals in the population, or they may be chosen randomly. Likewise, when migrants arrive at a deme, they may replace individuals randomly or they may replace the worst. Each of these decisions affects the speed of convergence, except when both the migrants and the individuals they replace are chosen randomly (Cantú-Paz, 1999a; 2000), which was the case used in the distributed panmictic algorithm. If a different migration policy is used, the multi-deme algorithm may converge faster, as we will see in Chapter 7.

The differences between the distributed panmictic population and fully-connected demes that communicate every generation with the maximal migration rate are very small, and we can expect that they reach solutions of the same quality (which can be predicted with the gambler's ruin model). If this is the case, then the calculations in Chapter 3 are appropriate for this bounding case.

The remainder of this chapter considers multi-deme GAs that use the *lower* bound of the migration frequency: migration occurs after the demes have converged (i.e., all the individuals in each deme are identical, not necessarily representing an optimal solution). After convergence, each processor partitions its population into r mutually exclusive sets, and exchanges the individuals of the i-th set with the i-th deme. The demes restart after migration, and execute the GA operations until they converge again. One advantage of this bounding case is that the communication costs are very low when individuals migrate after convergence because communications are very infrequent, and because it is sufficient to send one individual and replicate it as necessary at the receiving deme.

The time intervals between migrations will be called *epochs*. This section considers only the first two epochs of the algorithm; Chapters 5 and 6 extend the analysis to multiple epochs.

4.1   SUCCESS PROBABILITY AND DEME SIZE

Recall that the probability that a partition converges to the correct value in a GA with a single population is predicted by the solution to the gambler's ruin problem:

$$P_{bb} = 1 - \left(\frac{q}{p}\right)^{x_0},$$

where x_0 is the expected number of BBs present initially. When the demes converge the first time, a partition either has n_d copies of the correct BB with probability P_{bb}, or it has n_d copies of the wrong BB with probability $1 - P_{bb}$. After convergence each deme receives n_d/r migrants from every other deme. Some of those migrants contain the wrong BB, but some have the correct one. Therefore, after migration each partition has on average $n_d P_{bb}$ copies of the correct BB, which means that the second epoch starts from a better starting point than the first. To estimate the probability that the deme converges correctly at the end of the second epoch, the gambler's ruin model may be used again; we only need to replace x_0 with the new starting point as follows:

$$P_{bb_2} = 1 - \left(\frac{q}{p}\right)^{n_d P_{bb}} \tag{4.9}$$

Calculating this probability is the critical part of the modeling,[4] now we can use it to find the expected number of partitions correct in the best deme as

$$E(Q_{r:r}) = m P_{bb_2} + \mu_{r:r}\sqrt{m P_{bb_2}(1 - P_{bb_2})}. \tag{4.10}$$

This equation shows that there are two benefits from using multiple connected demes. As in the isolated case, the expected quality of the best deme increases by a factor of $\mu_{r:r}$, but we saw before that this is not a big difference. The major improvement comes from the expected quality in each deme $(m P_{bb_2})$ which is much greater than in the simple GA or the isolated demes, because the second epoch begins from a better starting point.

The required deme size for the fully-connected topology will be calculated next using a procedure similar to the one used for the isolated case. The first step is to calculate the relaxation of the quality required in each deme so that the best of the demes reaches the desired solution. This was already done in the previous section, and the result is denoted by $\hat{P}$ (Equation 4.3). The second step is to solve $\hat{P} = P_{bb_2}$ for the deme size, n_d.

We would like to use Equation 4.9, but the P_{bb} in the exponent depends on n_d, making it impossible to obtain a closed-form expression for n_d. Instead, Equation 4.9 has to be approximated and the deme size will be derived from the approximation. Equation 4.9 can be rewritten exactly as: $P_{bb_2} = 1 - (1 - c)^{n_d P_{bb}}$ where $c = 1 - q/p$, and in this form P_{bb_2} can be approximated as

$$P_{bb_2} \approx 1 - \exp(-c n_d P_{bb}). \tag{4.11}$$

Similarly, P_{bb} can be rewritten exactly as $P_{bb} = 1 - (1 - c)^{n/2^k}$ and approximated as $P_{bb} \approx 1 - e^{-cn/2^k}$. Using the first two terms of the Maclaurin series for $e^{-x} = 1 - x$, P_{bb} can be approximated roughly as

---

[4]Strictly speaking, it is incorrect to use the expected value of the count of correct BBs and iterate the GR model. Consider, for example, that we are ignoring the possibility that all the demes converged incorrectly. The next chapter will explain this problem in more detail, and will present a correct model. However, this section shows that the simple iterated model is an adequate approximation for two epochs, especially if we assume that there are many demes.

$P_{bb} \approx \frac{cn}{2^k}$. Substituting this form of P_{bb} into Equation 4.11 results in

$$P_{bb_2} \approx 1 - \exp\left(\frac{-c^2 n_d^2}{2^k}\right). \tag{4.12}$$

With this form of P_{bb_2}, we can now solve $\hat{P} = P_{bb_2}$ and find a deme-sizing equation:

$$n_d \approx \frac{\sqrt{-2^k \ln(1 - \hat{P})}}{1 - \frac{q}{p}}, \tag{4.13}$$

which can be approximated in terms of the domain signal and noise as

$$n_d \approx \sqrt{-2^k \ln(1 - \hat{P}) \pi m'} \frac{\sigma_{bb}}{2d}. \tag{4.14}$$

The deme size depends on the *square root* of $2^k \ln(1 - \widehat{P_{bb}})$ as opposed to the case for isolated demes where the deme size is directly proportional to this term. Although the approximation is coarse, this equation clearly shows that a parallel GA with migration needs much smaller demes, which in turn represent a substantial reduction of the time the GA uses in computations. However, the cost of communications will partially offset the reduction in computation time.

4.2   SPEEDUPS

We can estimate the time that each deme uses to communicate with the other $r - 1$ demes as $(r - 1)T_c$, and the time used in computations as $g n_d T_f$, where g represents the number of generations until convergence, n_d is the deme size, and T_f is the time required to evaluate each individual. Therefore, the execution time of the parallel program may be estimated as

$$T_p = g n_d T_f + (r - 1)T_c. \tag{4.15}$$

At this point, we can observe that as more demes are used there is a tradeoff between increasing communication cost and decreasing computations (because smaller deme sizes are needed). This tradeoff entails the existence of an optimal number of demes that minimizes the parallel time. The rest of this section deals with finding the optimum.

To optimize the parallel time, we could try to set $\frac{\partial T_p}{\partial r}$ to zero and solve for r to obtain the optimal number of demes. Unfortunately, the derivative cannot be solved analytically for r; thus, to make progress in the optimization of speedups we need to approximate the parallel deme size with a simpler expression.

We observed that plotting the parallel deme size against the number of demes on a log-log scale results in an almost-straight line, which means that the deme size can be approximated closely with a general power-law equation: $n = Ar^B$, where A and B are domain-dependent constants. The value of B may be computed as

$$B = \frac{\ln(n_1/n_2)}{\ln(r_1/r_2)},$$

where r_1 and r_2 are two deme counts, and n_1 and n_2 are the corresponding parallel population sizes (obtained by using r_1 and r_2 in Equation 4.13). The value for A can be obtained directly as $A = \frac{n_1}{r_1^B}$.

With this characterization of the parallel deme size, the computation time may be approximated as $gn_dT_f \approx gAr^BT_f$. Substituting this approximation into Equation 4.15 results in

$$T_p = gAr^BT_f + (r - 1)T_c. \tag{4.16}$$

Now we can set the derivative of T_p to zero and solve for r to obtain the optimal number of demes as

$$r^* = \left(-\frac{ABgT_f}{T_c}\right)^{\frac{1}{1-B}} = (-ABg\gamma)^{\frac{1}{1-B}}, \tag{4.17}$$

and the optimal deme size is $n_d^* = Ar^{*B}$.

The models of this section were validated with experiments using the same test functions of the previous section. Figure 4.2 shows the predictions and the experimental results of the parallel speedups using 4- and 8-bit trap functions. The parameters for the GAs were the same as for the experiments with isolated demes, and the same experimental procedure was used.

Both the predictions and the experimental results show an optimal speedup at approximately the same number of demes. Note that for the 4-bit trap function, the speedup is less than one for several deme counts, which means that the parallel algorithm takes longer to finish than the serial GA. This poor performance is mainly due to the expensive communications in our system, but it is also important to note that since the 4-bit problem can be solved with relatively small populations, the savings on computation costs are too small to compensate for the rapidly increasing costs of communications.

In the case of the 8-bit trap, the speedups are always greater than one for the range of demes used in the experiments. In fact, the parallel algorithm shows a significant advantage over the serial GA, even in our implementation with expensive communications. For this function, the

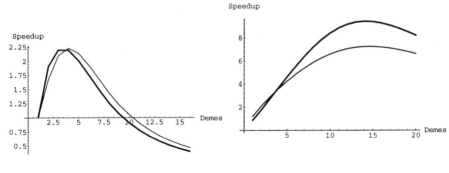

(a) 4-bit trap function with 20 BBs.   (b) 8-bit trap function with 10 BBs.

Figure 4.2. Speedups for fully-deceptive trap functions using 1 to 16 fully-connected demes. The quality demanded was 80% BBs correct. The thick lines are the theoretical predictions and the thin lines are the experimental results.

deme sizes required to find the required solution are much larger than for the 4-bit function, and the savings on the computation cost are enough to compensate for the expensive communications.

In contrast, the master-slave algorithm would perform poorly on these two problems because the computations are very simple. In the case of the 4-bit trap function, the single population size required to reach a solution with 80% of the BBs correct is $n = 110$ individuals. The optimal number of processors in a master-slave GA would be $\sqrt{n \frac{T_f}{T_c}} = \sqrt{110 \frac{0.034}{19}} = 0.44$, which means that a configuration with a single processor would be the fastest. The situation would be slightly better in the case of the 8-bit trap, because the population required to reach the required solution is much larger than with the 4-bit trap ($n = 1450$ individuals). For the 8-bit problem, the optimal number of processors would be $\sqrt{1450 \frac{0.061}{19}} = 2.13$, and the optimal speedup would be $2.13/2 = 1.0625$, only marginally better than a single population.

5   SUMMARY

The calculations presented in this chapter recognize that the design of parallel GAs is a complex problem, and that the choices of topologies, migration rates, number of demes, and their size are intimately related. To make progress on the deme-sizing problem without ignoring the other choices, the analysis used bounds on the topologies and migration rates.

The starting point of the analysis was to calculate the relaxation of the target quality per deme. Then, for each bounding case, we computed the expected quality of the best deme, and used the gambler's ruin model to derive deme-sizing equations. The sizing results were then used to estimate the execution time of the parallel GA.

The first result of this chapter is that if there is no communication between the demes, their sizes decrease very modestly, and the speedup is very small. On the other hand, when the demes communicate, there are great improvements in performance, because the deme sizes are much smaller. In this case, it is possible to estimate the number of demes and a corresponding deme size that maximize the speedup.

Moreover, the formulas for the optimal deme size and deme count can be adjusted to consider particular implementations and to predict the effect of improvements in hardware or software in the performance of parallel GAs. With these tools, it is possible to guide the developer to those aspects of the implementation that will make a greater impact on performance. The next chapters extend the analysis to consider multiple epochs, other topologies and reduced migration rates.

Chapter 5

MARKOV CHAIN MODELS
OF MULTIPLE DEMES

This chapter extends the models of the search quality of parallel genetic algorithms with multiple demes. The chapter considers three cases of increasing difficulty. It starts by considering the upper bounding case of topologies and migration rates that was used in the previous chapter. This case is the easiest to model, and it is used to introduce the methodology that will be applied to the more complex cases. The second algorithm considered here also has a fully-connected topology, but the migration rate may take any value. Finally, the chapter models algorithms with arbitrary topologies and migration rates that are more likely to be used in practice.

As in the previous chapter, the migration frequency is bounded: migration occurs after the demes converge. After migration, the migrants are incorporated randomly into the demes and the algorithm restarts. The time interval between migrations is called an epoch. Until now, we have considered only the first two, but this chapter considers any number of epochs. The objective of this chapter is to predict the solution quality after each epoch and also in the long run, when all the populations converge to the same solution and no further improvement is possible.

The critical observation in this chapter is that the probability that a deme will converge to the correct solution depends only on events of the previous epoch. This means that the algorithm that we are considering is a Markov chain, and this chapter uses well-known methods to study this type of stochastic processes.

The next two sections treat the fully-connected case. Section 1 examines the algorithm with the maximal migration rate, and Section 2 extends the analysis to lower migration rates. The models are generalized in Section 3 to consider arbitrary topologies and migration rates. Section 4 presents experiments that confirm the extended model. The chapter ends with a summary in Section 5.

1   FULLY-CONNECTED DEMES WITH MAXIMUM MIGRATION RATES

The previous chapter showed how to predict the quality of the solution at the end of the second epoch, assuming that the algorithm uses a maximal migration rate. The main idea was to use the expected number of correct BBs in a deme after migration, $x_1 = n_d P_{bb}(x_0)$, as the starting point of the gambler's ruin model.

This simple approximation results in reasonably good predictions after the second epoch, and one would be tempted to generalize the model to multiple epochs by estimating the expected number of BBs at the start of the τ-th epoch $(\tau > 0)$ as $x_\tau = n_d P_{bb}(x_{\tau-1})$, and iterating the gambler's ruin model. But this would be incorrect. We would not considering that the correct value of a partition may not appear in any of the demes, or it may be lost after some epochs. The *expected* number of BBs increases steadily over time, and after a few iterations, the probability of converging correctly would be 1, regardless of the population size or the number of demes.

For example, consider a fitness function formed by concatenating 20 copies of a 4-bit fully-deceptive trap function. Table 5.1 shows that after only eight (five) epochs, the iterated gambler's ruin model predicts that a parallel GA with demes of 16 (32) individuals will converge to the correct solution. This is not an accurate prediction of the behavior of parallel GAs.

1.1   MODELING WITH MARKOV CHAINS

To predict the quality of solutions found after an arbitrary number of epochs, we need to determine accurately the starting point of the random walk. In the case of maximum migration and fully-connected demes, the number of correct BBs at the start of an epoch depends only on how many demes converged correctly in the previous epoch. In particular, if i demes converged correctly and n_d is the deme size, each deme would start the current epoch with $\chi_i = \frac{i n_d}{r}$ copies of the correct BB, and the probability that it converges correctly is $P_{bb}(\chi_i)$. So, the problem consists on computing the number of demes i that have the right BB after each epoch (Cantú-Paz 1998b, 2000).

With the gambler's ruin model, we can calculate the probability that one deme converges correctly after the first epoch as $P_{bb}(x_0)$, where $x_0 = \frac{n_d}{2^k}$ is the expected number of correct BBs in a randomly initialized population. Since the demes evolved independently (there has not been any communication yet), at the end of the first epoch, the number of

Table 5.1. The iterated gambler's ruin model always converges to 1, regardless of the deme size (n_d) or the number of demes.

	Epoch	x_τ	$P_{bb}(x_\tau)$
	0	1	0.2144
	1	3.4	0.5668
	2	9	0.9024
$n_d = 16$	3	14.4	0.9894
	4	15.8	0.9990
	5	15.98	0.9999
	6	15.99	0.9999
	7	16	1
	0	2	0.3753
	1	12	0.9410
$n_d = 32$	2	30.11	0.9996
	3	31.99	0.9999
	4	32	1

demes that converged to the correct BB has a binomial distribution:

$$\mathbf{V}_1(i) = \binom{r}{i} P_{bb}^i(x_0)\, (1 - P_{bb}(x_0))^{r-i}. \qquad (5.1)$$

At this point, the demes exchange individuals and start the second epoch, but this time they have χ_i BBs initially. To calculate the probability of converging correctly after the second epoch we must consider all the possible outcomes of the first epoch:

$$P_{bb_2} = \sum_{i=0}^{r} \mathbf{V}_1(i) \cdot P_{bb}(\chi_i). \qquad (5.2)$$

Let $\mathbf{V}_\tau(i)$ denote the probability that exactly i demes converge correctly after the τ-th epoch. The expression above can be generalized and expressed as the vector product

$$P_{bb_\tau} = \mathbf{V}_{\tau-1}\mathbf{U}, \qquad (5.3)$$

where $\mathbf{U}(i) = P_{bb}(\chi_i)$. The challenge is to calculate the distribution of correct demes after an arbitrary number of epochs $(\mathbf{V}_\tau)$, and for this purpose we use Markov chains.

Markov chains are stochastic processes that can assume a finite number of states (distinct values) and satisfy the Markov property: the

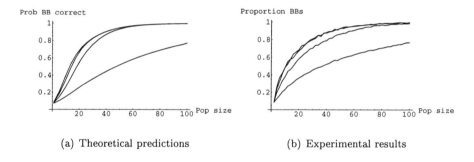

(a) Theoretical predictions   (b) Experimental results

Figure 5.1. Probability of converging to the correct BB after 1,2,3,and 4 epochs (from right to left).

probability of being in one particular state depends only on the previous state. For our purposes, the states of the chain represent the number of demes that converged to the correct BB in a given epoch. We can define a transition matrix with the probabilities of going from a state with i demes correct to a state with j demes correct as follows:

$$\mathbf{M}(i,j) = \binom{r}{j}(P_{bb}(\chi_i))^j(1 - P_{bb}(\chi_i))^{r-j}. \qquad (5.4)$$

Using the transition matrix, we can calculate the distribution of the number of demes that converge correctly after τ epochs as

$$\mathbf{V}_\tau = \mathbf{V}_1\mathbf{M}^{\tau-1}, \qquad (5.5)$$

and the probability of converging to the correct BB may be calculated with Equation 5.3.

Figure 5.1 presents an example of the predictions of Equation 5.3 after several epochs on four fully-connected demes. The example considers the same deceptive trap problems used in previous chapters, and the GAs used the same parameters as before. Contrast against the predictions of the iterated gambler's ruin example in Table 5.1. Note that the major improvement in quality comes at the second epoch, and therefore the calculations in the previous chapters are very significant for the design of parallel GAs.

1.2   PARALLEL DEMES IN THE LONG RUN

The example in Figure 5.1 also suggests that the probability of finding the correct BB converges to a fixed value after a few epochs. Another application of Markov chains is to calculate the long-run distribution of the number of demes that find the BB, that is $\lim_{\tau\to\infty}\mathbf{V}_\tau$. Substituting this distribution in Equation 5.3 gives the probability that, in the long run, the parallel GA finds the correct BB. The remainder of this section treats this issue, and also shows how to calculate the expected number of epochs until all the demes converge to the same solution.

First, recall the assumption made in Chapter 2 that crossover and mutation do not create or destroy significant numbers of correct BBs. This assumption implies that if the correct BB disappears from all the demes there is no way of recovering it. Likewise, when all the demes converge to the correct BB there is no chance of losing it. These facts are reflected in the transition matrix: the first row (corresponding to state 0, when no deme has the correct BB) is 1,0,0,...0, and the last row (state r, when all the demes have the correct BB) is 0,0,...,1. The states 0 and r are called absorbing or persistent states, and since there are no possible transitions between them, the chain has two closed absorbing sets. All the other states in the chain are called transient states.

The fundamental matrix method (Isaacson & Madsen, 1976) may be used to calculate the distribution of demes with the correct BB in the long run and the expected number of epochs until absorption. To use this method the states need to be reordered, and the transition matrix rewritten as

$$\mathbf{M} = \begin{pmatrix} \mathbf{P}_1 & 0 & 0 \\ 0 & \mathbf{P}_2 & 0 \\ \mathbf{R}_1 & \mathbf{R}_2 & \mathbf{Q} \end{pmatrix}, \tag{5.6}$$

where $\mathbf{P}_1$ and $\mathbf{P}_2$ are the submatrices with the transition probabilities within the two closed persistent sets, which in our case consist of a single state each (therefore, $\mathbf{P}_1 = \mathbf{P}_2 = 1$); $\mathbf{Q}$ is a submatrix with the transition probabilities within the transient states; and $\mathbf{R}_1$ and $\mathbf{R}_2$ contain the probabilities of going from each transient state to each of the persistent states.

The expected absorption time from each transient state i is given by the i-th element of

$$\mathbf{T} = \mathbf{N}\mathbf{1}, \tag{5.7}$$

where the matrix $\mathbf{N} = (\mathbf{I} - \mathbf{Q})^{-1}$ is sometimes called the fundamental matrix, $\mathbf{I}$ is the identity matrix, and $\mathbf{1}$ is a column vector of ones. We need to augment $\mathbf{T}$ with a zero at the beginning and a zero at the end, to account for the expected absorption times from state 0 and state r, respectively. Now, the mean time until absorption may be calculated by multiplying the initial distribution of demes with the correct BB (given by Equation 5.1) by the extended $\mathbf{T}$ ($\mathbf{T}'$) as follows:

$$\langle \tau \rangle = \mathbf{V}_1 \mathbf{T}'. \tag{5.8}$$

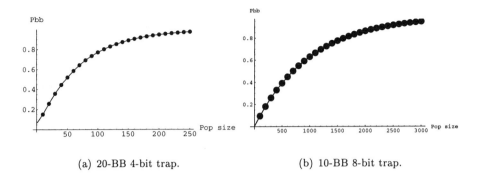

(a) 20-BB 4-bit trap.   (b) 10-BB 8-bit trap.

Figure 5.2. In the limit, a parallel GA with r fully connected populations using a maximal migration rate (dots) has the same chance of finding the solution as a simple GA with an aggregate population (continuous line).

The absorption probability from the transient state i to the persistent state l is given by the (i, l)-th entry of $\mathbf{NR}$, where $\mathbf{R}$ is the matrix formed with the elements of $\mathbf{R_1}$ and $\mathbf{R_2}$. Recall that $\mathbf{P_2}$ is the submatrix that contains state r, which represents the case where all the demes converge correctly. Thus, the distribution of probabilities, $\mathbf{A}$, of being absorbed into state r is given by the second column of $\mathbf{NR}$. We need to augment $\mathbf{A}$ with a zero at the beginning and a one at the end, to account for the chances of being absorbed from state 0 and state r, respectively. To find the probability of being absorbed at state r, we multiply the initial distribution of demes with the correct BB by the extended vector, $\mathbf{A'}$:

$$P_{bb_\infty} = \mathbf{V_1 A'}. \qquad (5.9)$$

Figure 5.2 presents plots of P_{bb_∞} using four demes with $0 \le n_d \le 100$ individuals each, and of P_{bb} (Equation 2.7) using a population size of $n = 4n_d$. The plots overlap perfectly, suggesting that the probability that r fully-connected demes of size n_d converge correctly in the long run is the same as the probability of success of a GA with a single population with rn_d individuals. This is important because it suggests that, *in the long run*, the solution's quality does not degrade or improve when a population is partitioned into smaller fully-connected demes that communicate with the maximum migration rate possible.

It is not immediately clear what would be the outcome if the populations communicate with a lower migration rate or a different topology. The following sections study the effects of these two parameters on the quality of the solutions.

2 ARBITRARY MIGRATION RATES

Using the maximal migration rate simplifies the calculation of the number of BB present in a deme after each epoch, because the contribution from all the demes is uniform. This section extends the calculations to cases with lower migration rates. The migration rate is denoted by ρ and represents the fraction of the population that migrates. The method used here is very similar to the one used in the previous section, but with lower migration rates, the initial number of BBs in a particular deme depends greatly on whether it converged correctly in the previous epoch.

For example, consider that in a given epoch, two out of three demes of a parallel GA converge correctly, and suppose that each population sends a fraction $\rho = 0.05$ of its individuals to the other two. At the start of the next epoch there are two possibilities for a particular deme. First, if it converged correctly in the previous epoch, then 95% of its individuals have the correct BB: 90% were already there, and it obtained 5% from the other correct deme. On the other hand, if the deme did not converge correctly, only 10% of the population would have the correct BB, contributed by the other two demes.

To reflect this situation, the Markov chain needs twice as many states as before. For each count of correct demes, the chain needs two states: one to represent the case when the major fraction of the deme contains the BB (because the deme converged correctly in the previous iteration), and another state to represent when the major fraction of the deme is incorrect. A convenient way to order the states is that states 0 to $r - 1$ represent the cases where the major fraction of the deme is incorrect, and states r to $2r - 1$ represent the cases where major fraction is correct. This ordering of the states is arbitrary, and any other ordering would be adequate. As before, there is one absorbing state for the case when all the demes converge incorrectly (state 0), and one for when all the demes converge to the correct BB (state $2r - 1$). The rest are transient states.

The initial distribution is

$$\mathbf{V}_1(i) = \begin{cases} \binom{r-1}{i}[P_{bb}(x_0)]^i \, [1 - P_{bb}(x_0)]^{r-i} & \text{if } i < r, \\ \binom{r-1}{i-r}[P_{bb}(x_0)]^{i-r+1} \, [1 - P_{bb}(x_0)]^{2r-i-1} & \text{if } i \geq r, \end{cases} \quad (5.10)$$

for $i \in [0, 2r - 1]$. The transition matrix becomes

$$\mathbf{M}(i,j) = \begin{cases} \binom{r-1}{j}[P_{bb}(\chi_i)]^j \, [1 - P_{bb}(\chi_i)]^{r-j} & \text{if } j < r, \\ \binom{r-1}{j-r}[P_{bb}(\chi_i)]^{j-r+1} \, [1 - P_{bb}(\chi_i)]^{2r-j-1} & \text{if } j \geq r, \end{cases} \quad (5.11)$$

where χ_i is the starting point of the random walk for each state i, and it depends on the migration rate ρ and on how many demes converged

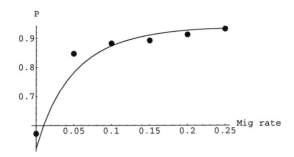

Figure 5.3. The probability of converging to the correct BB increases with higher migration rates. The theoretical predictions (continuous line) are compared against experimental results.

correctly:

$$\chi_i = \begin{cases} n_d\, i\, \rho & \text{if } i < r, \\ n_d\left((i-r)\rho + 1 - (r-1)\rho\right) & \text{if } i \geq r. \end{cases} \quad (5.12)$$

The probability of converging to the correct BB after τ epochs is given by $P_{bb_\tau} = \mathbf{V}_{\tau-1}\mathbf{U}$ (Equation 5.3), where $\mathbf{U}(i) = P_{bb}(\chi_i)$, and χ_i is defined as above.

Figure 5.3 illustrates the probability of reaching the correct solution as a function of the migration rate. The example uses four fully-connected demes with 50 individuals each; the test function is a 20-BB 4-bit trap problem; and only the first two epochs are considered. Note that the probability of success increases rapidly with higher migration rates.

As before, the fundamental matrix method may be used to predict the long-term behavior of the parallel GA with arbitrary migration rates. The states have to be reordered as in the previous section, and the calculations are similar, so we will not repeat them here. Figure 5.4 shows the probability that, in the long run, the parallel GA will converge to the correct solution as a function of the migration rate. The plot suggests that only a moderate migration rate is sufficient to reach the same solution as a simple GA with a aggregate population. Note that since all the individuals are the same when migration occurs, there are no cost penalties associated with higher rates: only one individual needs to be sent and it can be replicated any number of times at the receiving deme.

3   ARBITRARY TOPOLOGIES

The previous two sections showed that the modeling became more complex as the examined algorithms became more flexible. In the first case,

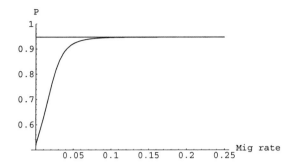

Figure 5.4. The long-run probability of converging to the correct BB increases rapidly with higher migration rates. The example considers four fully-connected demes, with 50 individuals each, working on a 20-BB 4-bit trap function. The horizontal line is the probability that four fully-connected demes with maximal migration (or a simple GA with 200 individuals) will eventually converge to the right BB.

when the migration rate was maximal, the only information required to calculate the number of BBs at the start of an epoch was the number of demes that converged correctly. But, when the migration rate was allowed to change, additional states were required to represent whether the local deme had converged correctly or not. The nature of the information represented by each state changed from a mere count of correct demes to include some additional spatial information (i.e., it became important to know *which* demes had the correct BB).

Additional spatial information is required when considering arbitrary topologies. In this case, it is not sufficient to know how many demes converged correctly in the previous epoch, but also *exactly* which ones. This information is represented in the states of the Markov chain, and therefore we expect to use many additional states. Since a deme can either have the correct BB or not, in a setup with r demes there are 2^r possible states. A natural representation of this information is to use a binary string s_i of length r for each state i. The k-th bit of the string, $s_i(k)$, corresponds to the k-th deme, and it is set to one if the deme converged correctly and to zero otherwise. The states of the Markov chain are numbered from 0 to $2^r - 1$ and can be conveniently labeled with the integers represented by the strings. For example, in a configuration with 8 demes, state 10 corresponds to the string $s_{10} = 00001010$ and represents the case where demes 1 and 3 converged correctly.

The construction of the transition matrix is not as straightforward as when the demes are fully connected. As before, the central idea of the modeling is to determine how many copies of the BB are present in a deme at the beginning of each epoch. The first step is to determine how many of the neighbors have the right BB, and for this we use a topology-dependent neighborhood function $N(a)$ that returns a set $\mathcal{N}_a$ with the indices of the neighbors of deme a. For example, in a bidirectional ring the neighbors of deme 1 are demes 0 and 2, so $\mathcal{N}_1 = N(1) = \{0, 2\}$. Since the states contain the information about which demes have the correct BB, it is easy to determine how many neighbors of a deme a converged correctly when the chain is at state i as

$$c_{i,a} = \sum_{k \in \mathcal{N}_a} s_i(k). \tag{5.13}$$

With this information, the number of BBs in deme a at the start of the epoch may be calculated as

$$\chi_{i,a} = n_d \left[c_{i,a}\, \rho + s_i(a)\, (1 - \delta\rho) \right], \tag{5.14}$$

where δ is the degree of the topology (i.e., the number of neighbors of a deme), and ρ is the migration rate. The first term above, $c_{i,a}\,\rho$, is the fraction of the deme with the correct BB that is contributed by the neighbors. The second term is about the correct BBs that were already present in the deme. When $s_i(a)$ equals one, deme a converged correctly in the previous epoch, and the fraction $1 - \delta\rho$ of the population that remained unchanged after migration contains the correct BB. If $s_i(a) = 0$, then the only correct BBs in the deme come from its neighbors.

The probability that deme a will converge correctly is $P_{bb}(\chi_{i,a})$, and so the probability of going from state i to state j is given by

$$\mathbf{M}(i, j) = \prod_{a=1}^{r} \left[s_j(a) P_{bb}(\chi_{i,a}) \;+\; (1 - s_j(a))(1 - P_{bb}(\chi_{i,a})) \right]. \tag{5.15}$$

For each value of a, only one term of the equation above is different than 0, depending on whether the a-th deme is correct or not in state j.

The distribution of states is given by $\mathbf{V}_\tau = \mathbf{V}_1 \mathbf{M}^{\tau-1}$ (Equation 5.5), and the probability of converging correctly is determined by Equation 5.3 ($P_{bb_\tau} = \mathbf{V}_{\tau-1}\mathbf{U}$). However, now

$$\mathbf{U}(i) = P_{bb}(\chi_{i,a}), \tag{5.16}$$

and $\chi_{i,a}$ is defined in Equation 5.14. Any choice of a may be used in this equation when the demes are connected by a vertex-transitive topology,[1] because on average all demes will have the same outcome.

---

[1] A vertex-transitive topology is one where the graph "looks the same" from all the nodes, like in rings, hypercubes, or regular meshes. A tree is not vertex-transitive, for example.

The initial distribution of states is given by

$$\mathbf{V}_1(i) = P_{bb}(x_0)^{u(s_i)}(1 - P_{bb}(x_0))^{r-u(s_i)}, \qquad (5.17)$$

where $u(s)$ is a function that counts the bits set to one in the string s.

The long-run probability of success may be found by reordering the states and using the fundamental matrix method, as was described in Section 1.

4 EXPERIMENTS

Several experiments were conducted to assess the accuracy of the model described in the previous section. The experiments used eight demes, and the test function was the same 20-BB 4-bit trap used previously. The GAs used pairwise tournament selection, two-point crossover with probability one, and no mutation. The results presented are the average over 100 repetitions.

The first set of experiments was designed to compare the quality of the solutions reached using different topologies. Figure 5.5 shows plots of the quality versus the number of epochs for a fully-connected topology and three topologies frequently used by practitioners: a uni-directional ring, a bi-directional ring, and a hypercube. Each of the eight demes has 30 individuals, and the migration rate was set to the maximum value possible for each topology: 50% for the uni-directional ring, 33% for the bi-directional ring, and 25% for the hypercube.

In all cases, the quality increases as more epochs are used, but the rate of increase depends on each topology. The uni-directional ring needs the most epochs to reach the highest quality possible—which is the same quality that simple GA with an aggregate population would reach—while the fully-connected topology realizes its full potential using the fewest epochs.

The experiments above suggest that, at any given time, topologies where the demes have more neighbors reach solutions of higher quality than sparse topologies: at any epoch the fully-connected topology reached the best solutions, while the uni-directional ring reached the worst. To visualize the effect of the degree more clearly, Figure 5.6 shows experiments where the degree varies while the deme size and migration rate are constant. The experiments used the four topologies used previously (with degrees 1, 2, 3, and 7). The experiments considered eight demes with 40 individuals each, and the quality was measured at the end of the second epoch. In the first experiment, the migration rate was set to 10% per deme (so the number of migrants received by a deme increases with the degree), and in the second experiment the total number of migrants was set to 20.

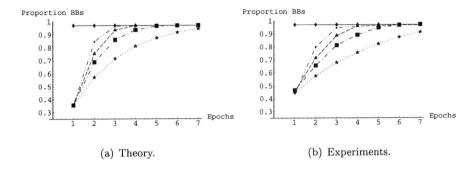

(a) Theory.   (b) Experiments.

Figure 5.5. Solution quality after several epochs. The graphs include data for uni- and bi-directional rings, a hypercube, and a fully-connected topology (from bottom to top, respectively). The horizontal line in both graphs is the prediction of the quality that would be reached by a simple GA with an aggregate population.

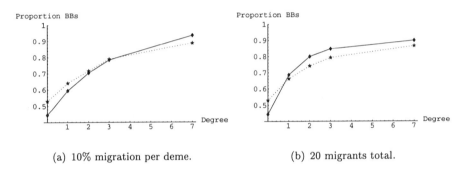

(a) 10% migration per deme.   (b) 20 migrants total.

Figure 5.6. Solution quality as a function of the degree of the topology. The continuous lines are the theoretical predictions, and the dashed lines are the experimental results.

In these two experiments, the quality increased quickly as the topologies became denser, but the marginal improvements are smaller. This is important because topologies with higher degrees have higher communication costs, and the marginal increase in quality may not be large enough to justify the additional cost. The next chapter explores this issue in detail, and shows how to optimize the execution time.

The next set of experiments was designed to test the accuracy of the models varying the migration rates. The experiments used rings (uni- and bi-directional) and a hypercube to connect eight demes with 50 individuals each. The migration rate varied from zero to the maximum rate possible in each topology, and the quality of the solutions was recorded at the end of the second, third, and fourth epochs. (During the first epoch the demes are isolated and their performance is equivalent to a

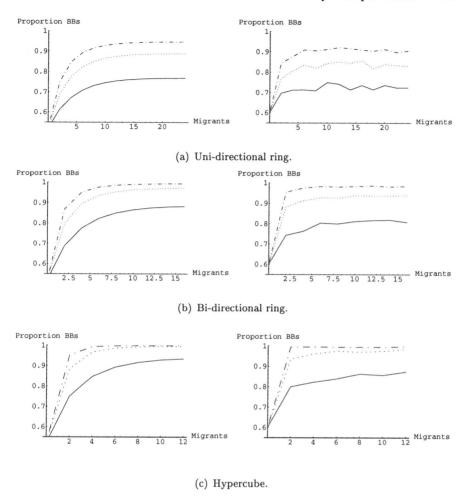

(a) Uni-directional ring.

(b) Bi-directional ring.

(c) Hypercube.

Figure 5.7.   Quality versus number of migrants. Each graph shows the quality using multiple migration rates after two, three, and four epochs (from bottom to top in each graph). The graphs on the left are theoretical predictions, and the graphs on the right are experiments.

migration rate of zero.) The results shown in Figure 5.7 confirm that the model accurately predicts the quality over a variety of migration rates and topologies. These experiments confirm the previous results that suggested that higher migration rates result in better solutions. As expected, the uni-directional ring reached the lowest-quality solutions, while the hypercube found the best.

5   SUMMARY

This chapter presented models that predict the expected solution quality of parallel GAs with multiple populations after any number of epochs and for any choice of deme size, deme count, topology, or migration rate. The basic idea was to model the parallel GAs as Markov chains to determine the number of correct BBs that are present in the demes at the beginning of each epoch. Then, the gambler's ruin model was used to predict the quality of the solutions.

The first algorithm that we examined was an upper bound on topologies and migration rates (the fully-connected case of the previous chapter). This case was the easiest to examine because all the demes have the same contributions to the next epoch. The second algorithm also had a fully-connected topology, but the analysis was extended to consider arbitrary migration rates. Finally, we examined arbitrary topologies and migration rates. The accuracy of the models was tested with computational experiments using one fully-deceptive test function and varying all the parameters of interest. In all cases, the predictions match closely the observed quality of the solutions after any number of epochs.

This chapter extended our understanding of multi-deme parallel GAs in several ways. First, we observed that the greatest gain in quality always occurs after the second epoch. This reinforces the significance of the calculations of the previous chapter that showed how to derive approximate closed-form expressions for the deme sizes and how to manipulate them to minimize the execution time.

The second contribution of this chapter is that the models and experiments suggest that, in the long run, the parallel GAs reach solutions of the same quality as a simple GA with a population equivalent to the aggregate of the demes. Partitioning the population does not degrade or improve the solution quality, as long as the migration rate is not very low. Furthermore, it appears that only a few epochs are necessary to reach the same solution as the simple GA.

An important observation is that the quality improves with higher migration rates and more neighbors per deme. Since migrations occur after the demes converge, the cost of communications is independent of the migration rate. However, higher degrees raise the cost of communications, and result in a tradeoff between increasing the quality or making the algorithm slower. The tradeoff suggests that, for an expected fixed solution quality, there is an optimal configuration that minimizes the execution time. The next chapter shows how to find this optimal configuration.

Chapter 6

MIGRATION RATES AND
OPTIMAL TOPOLOGIES

This chapter continues the study of multiple-deme parallel GAs. In previous chapters, we examined bounding cases of multiple-deme parallel GAs. The investigation of the bounding cases resulted in useful design guidelines, but those bounding configurations are not commonly used by practitioners because they are not scalable. In one case, when the demes are isolated, the improvements in quality are marginal and the total computational cost grows very fast. In the other case, when the demes are fully connected, the cost of communications quickly becomes impractical as more demes are used.

This chapter addresses the problem of designing scalable multiple-deme parallel GAs. Its goal is to find the configuration that reaches the desired solution in the shortest time possible. This chapter complements the Markov chain study of the previous chapter by deriving approximate models of the solution quality, which are used together with estimates of the execution time to find the optimal settings.

The models of this chapter assume that all the demes have the same number of neighbors, but there are no other restrictions on the topology or on the migration rates. As in previous chapters, the modeling focuses initially on the first two epochs, and it is later extended to any number of epochs.

The chapter is organized into four sections. Section 1 describes how the deme size, the migration rate, and the degree of the connectivity graph affect the chances that the desired solution is reached after the second epoch. This section also revisits the fully-connected topology, and shows that its optimal configuration is a good approximation of the optimal times of sparser topologies. Section 2 generalizes the results to multiple epochs. It shows that the solutions reached by different topologies with the same degree are almost identical, and then it focuses on one family of topologies to determine how the quality improves after arbitrary epochs. Next, the models are used to find an optimal configuration. Section 3 considers the long-run behavior of multiple demes. Finally, Section 4 summarizes the findings of this chapter.

1 DEGREE OF CONNECTIVITY

An important property of the connectivity graph between the demes is its *degree*, which is the number of neighbors of each deme. This chapter assumes that all the demes have the same degree, and we denote it as δ. The degree completely determines the cost of communications, and, as we shall see, it also influences the size of the demes and consequently the time of computations.

This section analyzes how the deme size, the migration rate, and the degree of the topology affect the probability that the parallel GA reaches the desired solution. The calculations of this section consider only the first two epochs of the algorithm, because closed-form expressions may be derived easily. The next section extends the modeling to multiple epochs. Some of these results were published before (Cantú-Paz, 1999b; Cantú-Paz & Goldberg, 1999; 2000).

The modeling has several steps. First, we compute how many copies of the correct BB are necessary to reach the target quality per deme, $\hat{P}$ (given by Equation 4.3). Recall that $\hat{P}$ is slightly smaller than the target solution quality, $\hat{Q}$, when multiple demes are used. Next, the probability that a given configuration brings together the critical number of BBs is calculated. The success probability is then used to derive a deme-sizing equation, which in turn is used to minimize the execution time.

The first step of the modeling is straightforward. To determine how many BBs, $\widehat{x_1}$, are needed to reach $\hat{P}$ at the end of the second epoch we may use the solution of the gambler's ruin problem (Equation 2.8). Making

$$\hat{P} = 1 - \left(\frac{q}{p}\right)^{\widehat{x_1}} \tag{6.1}$$

and solving for $\widehat{x_1}$ results in

$$\widehat{x_1} = \frac{\ln(1 - \hat{P})}{\ln\left(\frac{q}{p}\right)}. \tag{6.2}$$

The next step is to determine the probability that a deme receives at least $\widehat{x_1}$ BBs from its δ neighbors. The probability that one neighbor sends the right BB is the same probability that it converged correctly in the first epoch, and is given by P_{bb} (Equation 2.8). Assuming that all the neighbors of a deme use the same migration rate, ρ, then at least $\hat{\delta} = \frac{\widehat{x_1}}{\rho n_d}$ neighbors must contribute the correct BB. Since the demes have evolved in isolation until this moment, the probability of receiving at least $\widehat{x_1}$ BBs has a binomial distribution:

$$P_{x_1} = 1 - \sum_{i=0}^{\hat{\delta}-1} \binom{\delta}{i} P_{bb}^i (1 - P_{bb})^{\delta-i}, \tag{6.3}$$

which can be approximated as

$$P_{x_1} = 1 - \Phi\left(\frac{\hat{\delta} - \delta P_{bb}}{\sqrt{\delta P_{bb}(1 - P_{bb})}}\right), \tag{6.4}$$

where Φ denotes the CDF of a standard normal distribution. Figure 6.1 shows the results of experiments that illustrate the accuracy of P_{x_1}. The test problem used in this experiments is a 20-BB 4-bit trap function, and the figure shows the average of 100 independent runs.

With higher migration rates, fewer neighbors must contribute the right BB, and therefore it is more likely that the deme receives the critical number of BBs and succeeds to find the solution. This observation agrees with the results of the previous chapter that showed that solution's quality increased with higher migration rates.

Note that even if a deme receives less than $\widehat{x_1}$ BBs, it may still reach the right solution, because the deme itself could have converged correctly in the first epoch, and it may contain enough BBs to converge correctly again. Also, a deme may start the second epoch with less than $\widehat{x_1}$ BBs and converge correctly sometimes. However, we ignore these two possibilities and conservatively assume that a deme does not converge to the right answer if it does not receive at least $\widehat{x_1}$ BBs from its neighbors. Under these assumptions, P_{x_1} is the probability that at the end of the second iteration the deme will converge correctly.

There are different configurations that can bring together the critical number of BBs with the same probability (see Figure 6.2). Configurations with large demes and few neighbors have the same chance of success than some configurations with smaller demes but with more neighbors. This is the usual tradeoff between computation and computations: smaller demes require more neighbors to succeed. We would like to use the configuration that achieves the desired objective with the minimum cost.

The execution time of the parallel program is the sum of communication and computation times:

$$T_p = g n_d T_f + \delta T_c, \tag{6.5}$$

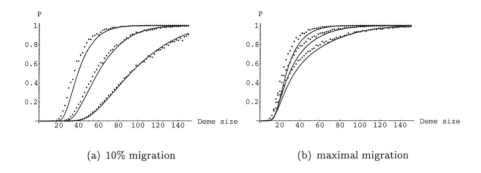

(a) 10% migration   (b) maximal migration

Figure 6.1. Plot of the probability of reaching the critical number of BBs required to find a solution with at least 16 out of 20 BBs ($\hat{Q} = 0.8$). The graphs show experimental results and the theoretical predictions using topologies with 1, 2, and 4 neighbors (from right to left in each graph) using different migration rates.

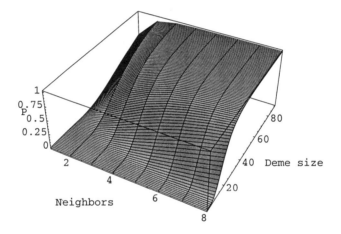

Figure 6.2. Plot of the probability of success with different configurations of deme sizes and number of neighbors. The migration rate in this example is 10%.

where g is the domain-dependent number of generations until convergence, n_d is the deme size, T_f is the time of one fitness evaluation, and T_c is the time required to communicate with one neighbor. T_c, T_f, and g can be easily determined empirically, but the required deme size depends on the degree of the topology, the migration rate, and the desired quality.

1.1   FINDING THE DEME SIZE

To find the deme size we need to make $P_{x_1} = \hat{P}$ and solve for n_d. First, the normal distribution of P_{x_1} has to be approximated as $\Phi(z) = (1 + \exp(-1.6z))^{-1}$ (Valenzuela-Rendón, 1989). With this approximation,

P_{x_1} becomes

$$P_{x_1} = 1 - (1 + \exp(-1.6z))^{-1}, \qquad (6.6)$$

where $z = \frac{\hat{\delta} - \delta P_{bb}}{\sqrt{\delta P_{bb}(1 - P_{bb})}}$ is the normalized number of successes. We may bound z by considering that the variance is maximal when $P_{bb} = 0.5$, and thus it becomes $z \geq \frac{2}{\sqrt{\delta}}(\hat{\delta} - \delta P_{bb})$ (In the remainder we conservatively ignore the inequality.). Additionally, P_{bb} may be roughly approximated as $P_{bb} \approx \frac{cn}{2^k}$, where $c = 1 - q/p$. Substituting this form of P_{bb} and $\hat{\delta} = \frac{\widehat{x_1}}{\rho n_d}$ into the bound of z gives

$$z = \frac{2}{\sqrt{\delta}}\left(\frac{\widehat{x_1}}{\rho n_d} - \delta \frac{cn_d}{2^k}\right).$$

Making the approximate form of $P_{x_1} = \hat{P}$ and solving for z yields the ordinate where the probability of success reaches the required value:

$$\hat{z} = 0.625 \ln\left(\frac{\hat{P}}{1 - \hat{P}}\right)$$

Making $z = \hat{z}$, solving for n_d, and simplifying gives the deme size:

$$n_d = \frac{2^{k-2}}{\sqrt{\delta}} \frac{\hat{z} + \sqrt{\hat{z}^2 + \frac{c\widehat{x_1}}{\rho 2^{k-2}}}}{c}. \qquad (6.7)$$

Observe that the deme size decreases with higher migration rates and as the number of neighbors increases, which is what we expected. For clarity, this deme-sizing equation may be rewritten in a more compact form by grouping all the domain-dependent constants into one (n_0) as follows:

$$n_d = \frac{n_0}{\sqrt{\delta}}. \qquad (6.8)$$

Now, the total execution time as given by Equation 6.5 may be easily optimized with respect to δ by making $\frac{\partial T_p}{\partial \delta} = 0$ and solving for δ to obtain

$$\delta^* = \left(\frac{g n_0 T_f}{2 T_c}\right)^{2/3}, \qquad (6.9)$$

and the optimal deme size can be found by substituting δ^* in Equation 6.7.

Figure 6.3 compares the theoretical predictions of the execution time with experimental results on a network of eight IBM workstations. In

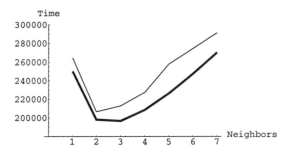

Figure 6.3. Comparison of theoretical (thick line) and experimental (thin line) execution times (in microseconds) of eight demes connected by topologies with different degrees.

this example, the fitness function is a 20-BB 4-bit trap, and the objective is to find a solution with at least 16 partitions correct. The time to evaluate a single individual is $T_f = 51$ microseconds, the communications time is $T_c = 29$ ms, and the number of generations until convergence is $g = 50$. The figure shows the average of 100 runs using pairwise tournament selection, two-point crossover with probability 1.0, and no mutation. The migration rate is $\rho = 0.1$.

1.2   FULLY-CONNECTED TOPOLOGIES REVISITED

Sometimes the magnitude of optimal degree will be greater than the number of demes, because it depends on the ratio of computation to communications, and this ratio may be arbitrarily large (see Equation 6.9). In those situations, the topology that is closest to the optimal and that is realizable with the available demes would be a fully-connected topology. This section revisits this bounding case, and shows that despite its poor scalability, the fully-connected topology may be a good choice to reduce the execution time.

The calculation of the optimal degree may be used to find an alternate expression for the optimal number of demes in a fully-connected topology. The idea is simply to realize that at some deme count, r, the optimal degree will be $\delta^* = r - 1$, which is the degree of the fully-connected topology. Solving for r gives the optimal number of demes,

$$r^* = \delta^* + 1. \tag{6.10}$$

Figure 6.4 has an example with the 20-BB 4-bit trap function used before. The example considers the same computing environment used in the experiments with fully-connected demes in Chapter 4. The fitness evaluation time is $T_f = 0.034$ ms, the communication time is $T_c = 19$

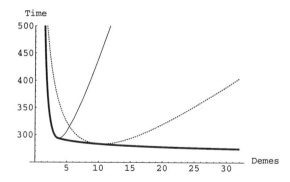

Figure 6.4. The execution time using the optimal degree decreases very slowly (bold line). It is bounded (and well approximated) by the optimal time of the fully connected topology (thin line). (See the text for an explanation of the points at $r = 2, 3$). The execution time of a topology of degree $r/4$ (dotted line) is plotted as an example.

ms, and $g = 50$ generations are required to converge. Only the first two epochs are considered to facilitate comparisons with the results of Chapter 4. The figure clearly shows that the time of optimally-configured topologies varies very slowly when more than r^* demes are used, and that the optimal execution time of the fully-connected case is very close to the optimal times of other topologies.

The optimal number of demes in the example ($r^* = 3.5$ that should be rounded to 4) agrees with the result in Chapter 4, where the optimum was found to be four demes. In this example, $\delta^* \approx 2.5$, which should be interpreted as $\delta^* = 3$. However, it is not possible to connect $r = 2$ or $r = 3$ demes together using more than $r - 1$ edges, and therefore the first two points in the plot of the optimal time correspond to a fully-connected topology.

Although the fully-connected topology cannot integrate many demes efficiently, its *optimal* configuration is a good choice to reduce the execution time. Optimally-configured topologies that use more demes reach solutions faster, but the reductions are not substantial. In fact, since the optimal time decreases very slowly when more than r^* demes are used, after that point the efficiency drops almost linearly with the number of demes. However, we shall see that optimally-configured topologies can reduce the execution time significantly after multiple epochs.

2   MULTIPLE EPOCHS AND CHOOSING A TOPOLOGY

The previous section showed how to find the optimal degree of connectivity that minimizes the execution time for a particular domain. However,

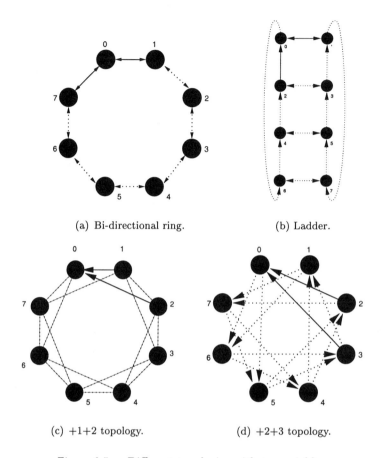

(a) Bi-directional ring.   (b) Ladder.

(c) +1+2 topology.   (d) +2+3 topology.

Figure 6.5.   Different topologies with two neighbors.

even with a fixed degree, there are many ways to connect the demes, and we still face the question of how to choose a particular topology. Certainly, if the algorithm is only executed for two epochs, it does not matter how the demes are connected, because only the immediate neighbors affect the search. But if more than two epochs are used, a deme would receive indirect contributions from other demes. The purpose of this section is to quantify the effect of those indirect contributions on the quality of the search, and to determine how to minimize the execution time after multiple epochs.

As an example of this problem, consider the topologies with degree $\delta = 2$ depicted in Figure 6.5. Figure 6.6 shows the results of experiments with a 20-BB 4-bit trap function on eight demes connected with these four topologies. The results are averaged over 100 repetitions at each deme size. The demes used pairwise tournament selection, two-point

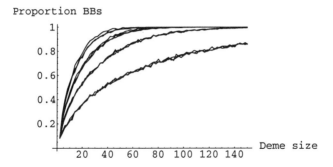

Figure 6.6. Average quality per deme after one, two, three, and four epochs (from right to left) using eight demes connected with different topologies of degree two.

crossover with probability 1.0, and no mutation. The migration rate was set to its maximal value of 1/3. The figure shows the proportion of correct BBs per deme after one, two, three, and four epochs. The quality of the solutions improves after successive epochs, and, as in the previous chapter, we can observe that the largest increase occurs after the second epoch. As one would expect, the results for different topologies during the first two epochs are indistinguishable, and the difference after three and four epochs is very small (it is statistically insignificant). Cantú-Paz and Mejía-Olvera (1994) observed a similar behavior on experiments when migration occurred at regular intervals. This observation will be used to derive a model of solution quality that depends on the degree of the connectivity graph and on the migration rate, but that ignores the specific topology. Before doing so, we first introduce the concept of the extended neighborhood of a deme.

2.1 EXTENDED NEIGHBORHOODS

To visualize how the choice of topology affects the quality of the search, imagine a tree rooted on a particular deme. The descendants of a node in the tree are the immediate neighbors of the deme it represents, and the τ-th level in the tree contains the demes that are reachable from the root deme after τ epochs. These demes form the extended neighborhood of the root and are taken into account only the first time that they are

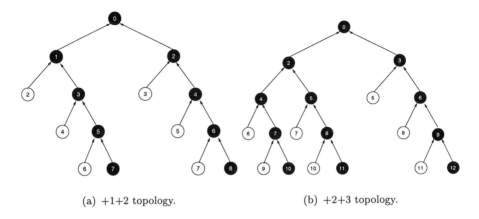

(a) +1+2 topology.   (b) +2+3 topology.

Figure 6.7.   Tree representations of the extended neighborhoods of demes in two different topologies of degree 2 with 16 demes. The black nodes represent the new members of the extended neighborhood after each epoch. The white nodes represent demes that already belong to the neighborhood, and they are not expanded to avoid clutter in the graphs.

reached.[1]   Figure 2.1 shows two such trees corresponding to the +1+2 and +2+3 topologies with 16 demes.

A simple way to bound the contribution from the extended neighborhood is to assume that the demes form panmictic groups as soon as they come in contact. In this view, after τ epochs the aggregate population size would be $r_\tau n_d$, where r_τ is the number of demes in the extended neighborhood after the τ-th epoch, and n_d is the size of each deme. Under this assumption, the solution quality would be given by $P_{bb}(r_\tau n_d)$. Of course, demes do not become panmictic as soon as they reach one another, and therefore the size of the extended neighborhood should be adjusted with a mixing coefficient $c_m < 1$. With the adjustment, the quality becomes $P_{bb}(c_m r_\tau n_d)$.

In any case, the simple approximation explains why those topologies where more demes contribute at each epoch reach slightly better results. To verify the hypothesis, experiments were performed with two topologies where exactly the same number of demes contribute after the first three epochs (r_τ is the same for both topologies for all values of τ). Eight demes were connected as an hypercube and a "cartwheel" (see

---

[1]We can define the extended neighborhood of a deme more formally. Consider a directed graph $G = (V, E)$, where V is the set of vertices that represent the demes, and E is the set of edges that represent connections between demes. The extended neighborhood of a deme v is the set $R_\tau = \bigcup_{i=0}^{\tau} a : a \xrightarrow{i} v$, where $a \xrightarrow{i} v$ denotes a path of length i from a to v. $r_\tau = |R_\tau|$.

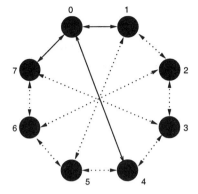

Figure 6.8. The "cartwheel" topology is similar to a bi-directional ring, but there is an extra link to the opposite deme.

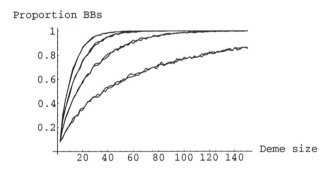

Figure 6.9. Average quality per deme after one, two, three, and four epochs using eight demes connected by two different topologies of degree three. The quality after all epochs is identical because the size of the extended neighborhoods are the same in both topologies.

Figure 6.8). As expected, the two topologies yielded identical results, which are plotted in Figure 6.9.

2.2 DESIGNING FOR MULTIPLE EPOCHS

The observation that topologies of the same degree reach almost identical solutions has an important implication: if an accurate predictor of quality can be derived for one topology, it would also be accurate for other topologies of the same degree.

Some topologies are easier to study than others because the size of their extended neighborhoods increases in a regular form. In particular, there are topologies where the size of the extended neighborhood increases linearly as $r_\tau = \delta(\tau - 1) + 1 = \delta\tau' + 1$. Examples of such topologies are the +1+2 binary topology depicted in Figure 6.5 and a +1+2+3 ternary topology. We will use this class of topologies to study the effect of the degree of the network on the solution quality after several epochs.

Using the simple model derived previously, the quality after τ epochs is $P_{bb_\tau} = P_{bb}(r_\tau n_d c_m)$. For simplicity, we use $n_\tau = r_\tau n_d c_m$ to represent the number of individuals in the extended neighborhood. The key to obtain an accurate quality prediction is to adjust n_τ with an appropriate c_m. We can deduce the value of the mixing coefficient by considering some of the properties it should have. For instance, n_τ should increase as τ grows, and when $\tau = 1$ the value of n_τ should be equal to n_d, because the demes are isolated during the first epoch. In addition, the previous section showed that the deme size $n_d \propto \frac{1}{\sqrt{\delta}}$ (Equation 6.8). Putting everything together, we may write n_τ as:

$$n_\tau = (\sqrt{\delta}\tau' + 1)n_d, \tag{6.11}$$

which means that $c_m = \frac{\sqrt{\delta}\tau'+1}{\delta\tau'+1} \approx \frac{1}{\sqrt{\delta}}$. Experimental tests were performed to assess the accuracy of this model. The experiments use eight demes connected by a +1+2 topology and the same experimental setup as previous experiments in this chapter. The deme sizes were varied, and the quality was measured at the end of the first four epochs. Figure 6.10 shows that the predictions of $P_{bb}(n_\tau)$ match very well the experimental results.

We may also compare the predictions of $P_{bb}(n_\tau)$ with the Markov chains model derived in the previous chapter. Figure 6.11 presents the same quality predictions as in Figure 6.10, and shows that for the +1+2 topology the difference between the two models is small. Another interesting test is to compare the two models on different topologies. Figure 6.12 compares the expected quality reached by eight demes of size 30 connected in three configurations: a uni-directional ring, a bi-directional ring, and a fully-connected topology. The migration rate is set to the maximal value possible in each topology, and the first seven epochs are considered. Again, the differences between the two models are small, and it appears that $P_{bb}(n_\tau)$ may be used confidently as a good predictor of solution quality.

The next step is to find a deme-sizing equation. The procedure is straightforward using the gambler's ruin model. Making $P_{bb}(n_\tau) = 1 - \left(\frac{q}{p}\right)^{n_\tau/2^k} = \hat{P}$ and solving for n_d results in

$$n_d = \frac{1}{\sqrt{\delta}\tau' + 1} \frac{2^k \ln(1 - \hat{P})}{\ln \frac{q}{p}}, \tag{6.12}$$

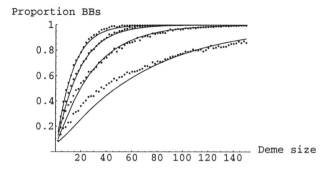

Figure 6.10. Theoretical predictions (line) and experimental results (dots) of the average quality per deme after 1, 2, 3, and 4 epochs (from right to left) using eight demes connected by a +1+2 topology.

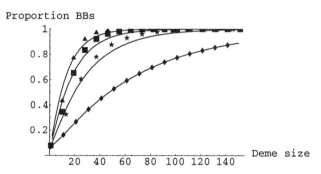

Figure 6.11. Comparison of the approximate (continuous lines) and the Markov chain models (dots). The graph shows the average quality per deme after 1, 2, 3, and 4 epochs (from right to left) using eight demes connected by a +1+2 topology.

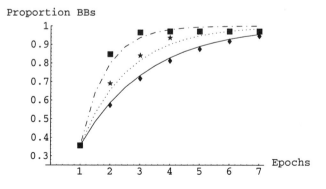

Figure 6.12. The graph compares the approximate (continuous lines) and the Markov chains models (dots) on three topologies: uni- and bi-directional rings and a fully connected topology (from right to left, respectively).

which can be rewritten in a much compact form by grouping all the problem-dependent constants (the second term above) into one constant n_0, so $n_d = \frac{n_0}{\sqrt{\delta\tau'+1}}$.

This form of the deme size with $\tau = 2$ is similar to the equation found in the previous section. With a closed-form expression for the deme size after multiple epochs, the execution time of the parallel GA may be easily minimized. In this case, the time is

$$T_p = \tau \left(g n_d T_f + \delta T_c \right). \tag{6.13}$$

To simplify the calculations, n_d may be approximated as $\frac{n_0}{\sqrt{\delta\tau'}}$. Making $\frac{\partial T_p}{\partial \delta} = 0$ and solving for δ gives the optimal degree of the topology as

$$\delta^* = \left(\frac{g n_0 T_f}{2\tau' T_c} \right)^{2/3}, \tag{6.14}$$

which is equivalent to the optimum found in the previous section when $\tau = 2$.

An interesting property of the optimal degree is that it depends very weakly on r. The dependency on r is in the $\ln(1 - \hat{P})$ term of n_0. In Chapter 4 we determined that $\hat{P}$ is approximately $\frac{Q}{m} - \frac{\sqrt{\ln r}}{\sqrt{2m}}$, so the dependency of the optimal degree on r is $O(\ln \ln r)$. This is important because if δ^* does not change much as more demes are used, then the execution time (Equation 6.13) would not change much either. However, we should not dismiss the algorithm's capability to decrease the execution time. After all, δ^* depends strongly on the number of epochs τ: both δ^* and the execution time decrease significantly as more epochs are used.

This raises another point: sometimes the choice of topology is restricted by the hardware. In this case, δ may be considered to be constant, and the execution time may be optimized with respect to τ. Making $\frac{\partial T_p}{\partial \tau} = 0$ and solving for τ gives the optimal number of epochs:

$$\tau^* = 1 + \sqrt{\frac{g n_0 T_f}{\delta^{3/2} T_c}}. \tag{6.15}$$

The corresponding deme size may be found by substituting δ^* (or τ^*) in Equation 6.12.

3   PARALLEL DEMES IN THE LONG RUN

This section focuses on an important property of parallel GAs with multiple populations. Namely, that in the long run, r demes of size n_d that repeatedly communicate with each other with the maximum migration rate possible, reach the same solution as a simple GA with a population with rn_d individuals. This property was established in Chapter 5. We denote as τ_c the critical number of epochs necessary to reach a solution as good as a GA with an aggregate population. Chapter 5 also showed how to use Markov chains to calculate τ_c, but although those calculations are accurate, they are not very easy to use. This section shows how to estimate τ_c using the simple models for solution quality derived in the previous section.

Recall that the execution time of the parallel GA depends directly on the number of epochs (Equation 6.13). By definition, when τ_c epochs are used, the size of the demes can be reduced to $n_d = \frac{n}{r}$, so the execution time becomes

$$T_p = \tau_c \left(\frac{gnT_f}{r} + \delta T_c \right). \tag{6.16}$$

Our objective is to minimize this time. All of the terms of this equation are known, except for τ_c. To derive an estimate of τ_c, note that $\lim_{\tau \to \infty} P_{bb}(n_\tau) = 1$, because n_τ grows without limit as more epochs are used, which is not correct. The derivation of n_τ is based on the concept of extended neighborhoods, but physically the size of the extended neighborhood is bounded by the sum of the sizes of all the demes (rn_d). Making $n_\tau = rn_d$, and solving for τ gives an approximation of the number of epochs it takes the algorithm to converge:

$$\tau_c = \frac{r-1}{\sqrt{\delta}} + 1. \tag{6.17}$$

Substituting the estimate of τ_c into Equation 6.16, making $\frac{\partial T_p}{\partial r} = 0$, and solving for r results in the optimal number of demes:

$$r^* = \sqrt{g \frac{\sqrt{\delta}-1}{\delta}} \sqrt{\frac{nT_f}{T_c}}. \tag{6.18}$$

Note that the second term also appears in the optimal processor count of master-slave parallel GAs, suggesting that asymptotically the two types of parallel GAs can use the same number of processors to reduce the execution time. However, the question of which algorithm is the fastest depends on the particular application. Users can use the equations presented in this book to estimate the execution time of the two types of parallel GAs and decide which one to use.

4   SUMMARY

This chapter extended the previous deme-sizing equations to consider configurations that are likely to be used by practitioners. The first part of the chapter described the relation between the deme size, the migration rate, and the topology's degree with the probability of success after two epochs. It showed how to find the configuration that optimizes the execution time while reaching a predetermined target quality. These calculations were also used to find an alternate expression for the optimal number of fully-connected demes (which was calculated initially in Chapter 4). Although this topology cannot integrate many demes, it can reduce the execution time substantially, and it may be competitive with other optimally-configured topologies.

The second part of the chapter generalized the results to multiple epochs. After multiple epochs, the topology is important because a deme receives indirect contributions from varying number of demes. Section 2 showed that different topologies with the same degree reach almost identical solutions after any number of epochs. A simple approximate model was derived to explain the small differences, but most importantly, the equivalence of topologies with the same degree facilitated the derivation of a model of solution quality. The quality model was transformed into an accurate deme-sizing equation, which in turn was used to minimize the execution time.

When the topology is fixed and the algorithm is executed until all the populations converge to the same solution, the optimal number of populations was found to be $O(\sqrt{\frac{nT_f}{T_c}})$, which is asymptotically the same as parallel versions of GAs with a single population. This result suggests that, regardless of their type, parallel GAs can integrate large numbers of processors and reduce significantly the execution time of many practical applications.

Chapter 7

MIGRATION, SELECTION PRESSURE, AND SUPERLINEAR SPEEDUPS

The previous chapters examined algorithms where migration occurred after the demes converged to a unique solution. This chapter examines algorithms where migration occurs every generation, which is the upper bound of the frequency of migrations. The chapter investigates the effect of the policy used to select migrants and the individuals that they replace at the receiving deme. This was not an issue on the algorithms examined before, because all the individuals of a deme were identical. It is known that when migrations occur before convergence, selecting the emigrants and replacements based on their fitness may increase the selection pressure (Whitley, 1993b; Whitley et al., 1999; Cantú-Paz, 1999b), but the impact of the migration policy on the algorithm's convergence is not well understood. The objective of this chapter is to quantify accurately the selection pressure caused by migration.

Understanding the effect of migration on the selection pressure is important, because the selection pressure influences significantly the speed of convergence of the algorithm. Excessively slow or fast convergence rates may cause the search to fail (Goldberg et al., 1993; Thierens & Goldberg, 1993). If selection is too weak, the population may drift aimlessly for a long time, and the quality of the solutions found is not likely to be good. On the other hand, rapid convergence is desirable, but an excessively fast convergence may cause the GA to converge prematurely to a suboptimal solution. In addition, the selection intensity is related to the optimal mutation rate and to the population size (Mühlenbein & Schlierkamp-Voosen, 1994; Bäck, 1996), as we saw in Chapter 2.

This chapter also offers a principled explanation to the frequent claims of superlinear speedups in parallel GAs. These controversial claims imply that the parallel GA requires less total effort to reach the same solution than a serial GA (Punch, 1998). However, we are left with a perplexing question: What caused the reduction in the required work?

The answer offered by this chapter is that convergence is accelerated by the additional selection pressure caused by some migration policies.

This chapter examines two basic alternatives to select the individuals that emigrate from a deme: choosing individuals randomly or based on their fitness using any selection method. Likewise, existing individuals in the receiving deme can be replaced randomly or according to their fitness.[1] Each combination of migrant selection and replacement policies causes a different selection pressure, and this chapter examines this effect using two different and complimentary approaches: calculating the takeover times and the selection intensities.

As was mentioned above, the calculations assume that migration occurs every generation. Less frequent migrations have a lower impact on the convergence of the algorithm. The calculations also assume that the migrants are copies of the individuals selected to migrate, which is the most common form of migration in GAs.[2]

The next section reviews common selection methods and explains intuitively the concept of selection pressure. Section 2 briefly summarizes previous work on takeover times for simple GAs, and it extends the calculations to consider four migration policies. The calculation of the selection intensity caused by different migration policies is in Section 3, and the results of experiments that validate the accuracy of the models are in Section 4. Section 5 has a brief discussion of superlinear speedups and illustrates how some of them can be explained by an increase in selection pressure. Section 6 examines the effect of migration on the variance and the higher cumulants of the fitness distribution. Finally, Section 7 summarizes the chapter.

1   SELECTION PRESSURE

Evolutionary algorithms use many different mechanisms to select the parents of the next generation. Selection methods can be classified roughly into two groups: fitness-proportionate and rank-based selection.

Fitness-proportionate methods select individuals probabilistically depending on the ratio of their fitness and the average fitness of the pop-

---

[1] Pettey, Leuze, and Grefenstette (1987) recognized that the replacement of existing individuals can also be based on their similarity with the incoming ones. The similarity can be measured in any way, for example using the Hamming distance. This chapter only considers selection and replacement based on fitness.

[2] Sprave (1999) distinguished between migration and pollination models. Sprave noted that in a proper simulation of migration, the migrants are deleted from their original population (i.e., the individuals *move* from one population to another), while in a pollination model the migrants are copies. Strictly speaking, we are considering pollination models, but we shall continue to use the term migration to conform with the common terminology in the field.

ulation. These methods are amongst the earliest methods used in GAs. Some examples are roulette-wheel selection (or also called proportionate selection) (Holland, 1975), stochastic remainder selection (Booker, 1982), and stochastic universal selection (Baker, 1987). Roulette-wheel selection uses a simulated roulette wheel with slots that are sized according to the fitness of each individual. The roulette is spun once for each individual to be selected. The other schemes were proposed to reduce the stochastic error associated with spinning the roulette wheel numerous times.

Some common rank-based selection methods are linear ranking (Baker, 1985), tournament selection (Brindle, 1981), $(\mu \dagger \lambda)$ selection (Schwefel, 1981), and truncation selection (Mühlenbein & Schlierkamp-Voosen, 1993). In linear ranking selection, individuals are selected with a probability that is linearly proportional to the rank of the individuals in the population. The desired expected number of copies of the best (n^+) and worst (n^-) individuals are supplied as parameters to the algorithm. In tournament selection, a random sample of s individuals is obtained (with or without replacement), and the best individual from the sample is selected. The process is repeated until the mating pool is filled. In $(\mu + \lambda)$ selection, λ offspring are created from μ parents, and the μ best individuals out of the union of parents and offspring are selected. In (μ, λ) selection $(\lambda \geq \mu)$, the μ best offspring are selected to survive. Truncation selection selects the top $1/\tau$ of the population and creates τ copies of each individual. It is equivalent to (μ, λ) selection with $\mu = \lambda/\tau$.

All of these selection mechanisms have the same purpose of creating more copies of the individuals with higher fitness than of those with low fitness, but they differ in the manner in which they allocate copies to the fittest individuals. Intuitively, a selection method has a higher selection pressure than another if it makes more copies of the best individuals, thereby eliminating more rapidly the low-fit individuals. A strong selection method reaches equilibrium faster than a weaker method, but in general, it also sacrifices genetic diversity that may be needed to find an adequate solution. The parameters of the selection methods regulate the selection pressure; we shall see that the parameters of migration also affect the selection pressure.

The speed of convergence of different selection schemes was first studied by Goldberg and Deb (1991), who introduced the concept of takeover time. The takeover time is the number of generations that selection requires to replicate a single individual of the best class until the population is full. The next section extends Goldberg and Deb's analysis to consider different migration policies. Later, Mühlenbein and Schlierkamp-Voosen (1993) used concepts from population genetics to study convergence properties of a particular GA, and introduced the concept of selection intensity to study the convergence of selection schemes. Of course, many others have studied and compared different selection methods used in GAs (for example, see Bäck (1994b) and Hancock (1997)).

2   TAKEOVER TIMES

This section is based on Goldberg and Deb's (1991) analysis of the takeover times of tournament selection, but similar calculations may be performed for other selection schemes. This section considers a simplified population model with only two classes of individuals: good and bad. We may think of the good individuals as representatives of the global solution, while the bad individuals are any other lesser solution. For simplicity, we consider that the migrants are either the best individuals in a deme or are chosen randomly. Similarly, the only replacement policies that we consider are to delete individuals randomly or to delete the worst. It should be noted that the calculations of takeover time consider only the effect of selection on the growth of good solutions and ignore other operators such as recombination and mutation.

Let P_t denote the proportion of good individuals in the population at time t, and $Q_t = 1 - P_t$ denote the proportion of bad individuals. In the particular case of tournament selection of size s, a bad individual will survive only if all the participants in the tournament are bad:

$$Q_{t+1} = Q_t^s. \tag{7.1}$$

Substituting $P = 1 - Q$ gives the proportion of good individuals:

$$P_{t+1} = 1 - (1 - P_t)^s. \tag{7.2}$$

The extensions below assume that migration occurs every generation, and that it occurs after selection, so its effect may be accounted for by adding a policy-dependent term to Equation 7.2 (Cantú-Paz, 1999b).

The simplified analysis of this section does not consider the origin of good migrants. For example, the analysis does not distinguish if a deme receives ten good migrants from one neighbor or five good migrants from two neighbors. Previous chapters have shown that the topology is one of the most important parameters of migration, but the takeover time calculations are not concerned with obtaining a good solution or with minimizing the communications. Here we are interested in investigating how fast a good solution dominates a population once it is found. Subsequent sections follow a different approach that makes fewer simplifying assumptions about the population model and the topology of communications. However, the qualitative observations made possible by the simple takeover time calculations will remain valid.

Out of the four migration policies, the easiest case to model is when good migrants replace bad individuals. With this policy, on every generation the proportion of good individuals increases by the migration rate ρ (which is the fraction of the population that migrates). Therefore, a difference equation for this case can be obtained easily, just by adding ρ to Goldberg and Deb's equation (Equation 7.2):

$$P_{t+1} = 1 - (1 - P_t)^s + \rho. \tag{7.3}$$

In the case where good individuals migrate and the replacements are chosen randomly, the migrants may replace good or bad individuals. If good migrants replace good individuals, then the proportion of good individuals in the receiving deme remains unchanged. Thus, we are interested in calculating how many bad individuals are replaced. The probability of replacing bad individuals is equal to their proportion in the population after selection, $Q_{t+1} = Q_t^s = (1 - P_t)^s$, and therefore the proportion of bad individuals that is replaced by the good migrants is $\rho(1 - P_t)^s$. Adding this to Equation 7.2 we obtain:

$$P_{t+1} = 1 - (1 - P_t)^s + \rho(1 - P_t)^s. \tag{7.4}$$

We can use a similar idea to examine the case when random migrants replace bad individuals. The proportion of good individuals in the receiving deme will increase by the good migrants, so we are interested in calculating how many migrants are good. Since migrants are chosen uniformly at random, the proportion of good migrants is the same as the proportion of good individuals present in a deme, $1 - (1 - P_t)^s$. Therefore, the proportion of good individuals at the receiving deme is incremented by the good migrants as follows:

$$\begin{aligned} P_{t+1} &= 1 - (1 - P_t)^s + \rho(1 - (1 - P_t)^s) \\ &= (1 + \rho)(1 - (1 - P_t)^s). \end{aligned} \tag{7.5}$$

When random migrants replace random individuals the proportion of good individuals in each deme is expected to be the same, so this migration policy does not have any effect on the takeover times.

To find the takeover times of the different migration policies, we simply iterate the difference equations obtained above and count the number of iterations until P_t reaches or exceeds 1. The starting point for the equations is $P_0 = 1/n$ (there is a single good individual in the population). Figure 7.1 shows the takeover times in demes with $n = 10000$ individuals and pairwise tournament selection ($s = 2$). The plots illustrate how the convergence is faster as the migration rate increases, and that the fastest convergence occurs when good migrants replace bad

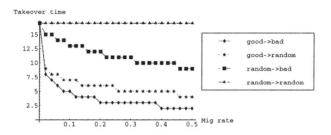

Figure 7.1. Takeover times using different migration policies and varying the migration rate.

individuals, which is a frequently-used migration policy (e.g., (Grefenstette, 1981; Tanese, 1987; Mühlenbein, 1991; Lin et al., 1997)). The slowest convergence occurs when both migrants and replacements are chosen randomly. A GA with a single population would converge in exactly the same time as this case.

These simple calculations suggest that the difference between the fastest and slowest convergence times is quite large, and therefore the migration policy must be taken into account when designing parallel GAs. The analysis also suggests that the choice of migrants is a greater factor in the convergence speed than the choice of replacements. We will observe a similar behavior in the next sections.

3   SELECTION INTENSITY

This section follows a different approach to estimate the convergence times of parallel GAs. The assumptions used here are more realistic than in the previous section, and the results are very accurate predictions of the convergence time. First, the concept of selection intensity is defined and closed-form expressions for the selection intensity of common selection methods are provided as a reference. Then, the additional selection intensity caused by migration is calculated, and we shall see how these values can be used to predict the convergence times. The next section verifies empirically the accuracy of the predictions.

The first observation needed to calculate the intensity of a selection method is that the average fitness of the individuals that are selected to survive is greater than the average fitness of the population. The magnitude of this increase depends on the selection method being used, and it can be quantified as the *selection differential*:

$$s^t = \bar{f}_s^t - \bar{f}^t, \tag{7.6}$$

Table 7.1. Selection intensity for common selection schemes.

Selection Method	Parameters	I
Tournament	s	$\mu_{s:s}$
(μ, λ)	μ, λ	$\frac{1}{\mu} \sum_{i=\lambda-\mu+1}^{\lambda} \mu_{i:\lambda}$
Linear Ranking	n^+	$(n^+ - 1)\frac{1}{\sqrt{\pi}}$
Proportional	σ_t, μ_t	σ_t / μ_t

which is the difference between the mean fitness of the selected individuals, $\bar{f}_s^t$, and the mean fitness of the population, $\bar{f}^t$ (Mühlenbein & Schlierkamp-Voosen, 1993). The superscript t denotes the generation number. Assuming that the fitness of the population has a normal distribution, the selection differential can be calculated as

$$s^t = I\sigma_t, \tag{7.7}$$

where σ_t is the standard deviation of the population at time t, and the factor I is the *selection intensity*. The selection intensity of some common selection schemes has been calculated analytically. Bäck (1995) and Miller and Goldberg (1995) independently derived the selection intensity for tournament selection, and Bäck (1995) also derived I for (μ, λ) selection. Blickle and Thiele (1996) calculated the intensity of linear ranking, and Mühlenbein and Schlierkamp-Voosen (1993) calculated I for proportional selection. Table 7.1 contains some of the known selection intensities (adapted from (Miller & Goldberg, 1996)). Note that I is independent of the distribution of the current population, except for proportional selection.

Calculating the standard deviation is more complicated, as it depends on the fitness function. For the case of a l-bit one-max function, uniform crossover (Syswerda, 1989) creates an approximately binomial fitness distribution with success probability P_t, where P_t is the proportion of bits set to one in generation t. Therefore, the standard deviation may be calculated as (Mühlenbein & Schlierkamp-Voosen, 1993; Thierens & Goldberg, 1994)

$$\sigma_t = \sqrt{l \, P_t(1 - P_t)}. \tag{7.8}$$

The selection differential $\bar{f}^{t+1} - \bar{f}^t = \sigma_t \cdot I$ can be written as

$$P_{t+1} - P_t = \frac{I}{\sqrt{l}} \sqrt{P_t(1 - P_t)}. \tag{7.9}$$

This can be approximated as a differential equation that can be solved to obtain the proportion of correct bits at time t as

$$P_t = 0.5 \left(1 + \sin \left(\frac{I}{\sqrt{l}} t + \arcsin(2P_0 - 1) \right) \right), \qquad (7.10)$$

where P_0 is the initial proportion of bits correct. In the case of the one-max function this is usually 0.5. Assuming that the population is large enough to converge to the optimum, the number of generations until convergence can be calculated making $P_t = 1$ and solving for t to obtain

$$G = \left(\frac{\pi}{2} - \arcsin(2P_0 - 1) \right) \frac{\sqrt{l}}{I}, \qquad (7.11)$$

which in the usual case when $P_0 = 0.5$ simplifies to $G = \frac{\pi}{2} \frac{\sqrt{l}}{I}$. We shall use the two equations above to verify the calculations of the selection intensity caused by migration.

The selection intensity is very convenient to compare different selection methods, and, as was mentioned above, it is related to the optimal population size and mutation probabilities. However, the study of selection intensity has some limitations that we must keep in mind. For instance, the selection intensity is only about the mean fitness of the population, and we ignore the variance and the higher moments. Although Section 6 will alleviate this problem, we are still considering only "macroscopic" variables about the fitness distribution, and we ignore other variables such as the diversity at the chromosome level.

Perhaps a more serious limitation is that the selection intensity ignores the effects of the operators on the fitness. This is an challenging topic for future research. In addition, we ignore the possibility that the search can fail: in this chapter we assume that the population is large enough to converge to the optimum, which can be facilitated following the suggestions of the previous chapters.

3.1   MIGRATION AND SELECTION INTENSITY

The remainder of the section follows closely the notation and method used by Bäck (1995) in his study of (μ, λ) selection. This should not imply that fitness-based migration is equivalent to (μ, λ) selection. Bäck's paper provides a good framework and some useful approximations that we adapt here for our own purposes.

To calculate the selection intensity, we must calculate the selection differential between the mean fitness of a deme after migration, $\bar{f}'$, and before migration, $\bar{f}$ (Cantú-Paz, In press):

$$s = \bar{f}' - \bar{f}. \qquad (7.12)$$

We drop the generation superscript because all the events described here occur in the same generation.

The average fitness before migration is simply $\bar{f} = \frac{1}{n}\sum_{i=1}^{n} f_i$, where f_i is the fitness of the i-th individual of the population in the current generation. The average fitness after migration can be written as a weighted sum of the average fitness of the migrants and the average fitness of the individuals that survive migration (i.e., are not replaced by migrants). Let δ denote the degree of the topology (the number of neighbors of a deme), and $m = \rho n$ the number of migrants from *one* deme. We can write

$$\bar{f}' = \frac{1}{n}\left(\delta m \bar{f}_{\mathrm{mig}} + (n - \delta m)\bar{f}_{\mathrm{sur}}\right), \qquad (7.13)$$

where $\bar{f}_{\mathrm{mig}}$ is the mean fitness of migrants from one deme, and $\bar{f}_{\mathrm{sur}}$ is the mean fitness of the $(n - \delta m)$ survivors. Similarly we can write

$$\bar{f} = \frac{1}{n}\left(\delta m \bar{f} + (n - \delta m)\bar{f}\right). \qquad (7.14)$$

Grouping similar terms, we can decompose the selection differential into two parts. One that corresponds to the selection of emigrants s_e and another that corresponds to the selection of replacements s_r:

$$\begin{aligned} s &= s_e + s_r \\ &= \frac{1}{n}\delta m(\bar{f}_{\mathrm{mig}} - \bar{f}) + \frac{1}{n}(n - \delta m)(\bar{f}_{\mathrm{sur}} - \bar{f}). \end{aligned} \qquad (7.15)$$

By writing the selection differential in this way, we can separate the calculation of the selection intensity into two independent steps. As in the previous section, we focus our attention to the cases when the best individuals are chosen deterministically to migrate and when migrants are chosen randomly. We also examine the cases when the worst or random individuals at the receiving deme are deleted.

The major assumption that we make is that the fitness values of the population, f_i, can be interpreted as samples of random variables, F_i, with a common distribution. We may arrange the random variables in increasing order as

$$F_{1:n} \leq F_{2:n} \leq \ldots \leq F_{n:n}.$$

These are the order statistics of the F_i variables, and we shall use them to calculate the average fitness of the emigrants and the survivors. Without loss of generality, we assume a maximization problem and normalize the random variables as

$$Z_{i:n} = \frac{F_{i:n} - \bar{f}}{\sigma}. \qquad (7.16)$$

The mean fitness of the $m = \rho n$ best individuals selected to migrate from *one* deme is

$$\bar{f}_{\text{mig}} = \frac{1}{m} \sum_{i=n-m+1}^{n} E(F_{i:n}), \qquad (7.17)$$

which may be rewritten in terms of the normalized variables as

$$\begin{aligned}
\bar{f}_{\text{mig}} &= \frac{1}{m} \sum_{i=n-m+1}^{n} (E(Z_{i:n})\sigma + \bar{f}) \\
&= \sigma \cdot \frac{1}{m} \sum_{i=n-m+1}^{n} E(Z_{i:n}) + \bar{f}.
\end{aligned} \qquad (7.18)$$

Now, we can calculate the selection differential caused by the migrants as

$$s_e = \frac{\delta m}{n}(\bar{f}_{\text{mig}} - \bar{f}) = \frac{1}{n} \cdot \sigma \cdot \delta \sum_{i=n-m+1}^{n} E(Z_{i:n}). \qquad (7.19)$$

Since the selection differential is also defined as $s = I \cdot \sigma$ (Equation 7.7), the selection intensity caused by selecting the best individuals to emigrate is

$$I_e = \frac{1}{n} \cdot \delta \cdot \sum_{i=n-m+1}^{n} E(Z_{i:n}). \qquad (7.20)$$

The expected value of the i-th order statistic of a sample of size n is defined as

$$\mu_{i:n} = E(Z_{i:n}) = n \binom{n-1}{i-1} \int_{-\infty}^{\infty} z\phi(z)\Phi^{i-1}(z)[1 - \Phi(z)]^{n-i}dz, \qquad (7.21)$$

where $\phi(z)$ and $\Phi(z)$ are the PDF and CDF of the distribution of fitness, respectively. For some distributions, we can use tables to find the expected values of the normalized order statistics (Harter, 1970). For instance, if the fitness has a standard normal distribution with $\phi(z) = \exp(-z^2/2)/\sqrt{2\pi}$ and $\Phi(z) = \int_{-\infty}^{z} \phi(x)dx$, the values of $\mu_{i:n}$ for $n \leq 400$ are readily available (Harter, 1970). Nevertheless, computing the sum in Equation 7.20 can be tedious, but fortunately the following approximation exists[3] (Burrows, 1972; Bäck, 1995):

$$\sum_{i=n-m+1}^{n} \mu_{i:n} \approx n\phi(\Phi^{-1}(1 - \rho)), \qquad (7.22)$$

---

[3]Bäck shows that for $n > 50$ the approximation is indistinguishable from the real values.

and therefore Equation 7.20 can be approximated as

$$I_e \approx \delta\phi(\Phi^{-1}(1-\rho)). \tag{7.23}$$

It is important to realize that the selection intensity is an adimensional quantity that does not depend on the fitness function or on the generation. The assumption of normality was only used in the final approximation; the calculations are valid for any distribution as long as $E(F_{i:n})$ may be computed (by substituting the appropriate PDF and CDF in Equation 7.21).

In the case where individuals are chosen randomly to emigrate, the expected fitness of the migrants is the same as the mean fitness of the population, and therefore the selection differential is $s = \bar{f}_{\mathrm{mig}} - \bar{f} = 0$, and there is no additional selection intensity ($I_e = 0$). However, there may be an increase in the overall selection intensity if the migrants replace the worst individuals in the target deme. The replacement of individuals is treated in the following paragraphs.

Replacing the *worst* individuals in a deme with migrants causes an increase in the average fitness of the deme. In a manner similar as above, we can calculate the mean fitness of the individuals that survive (i.e., are not replaced by the δm migrants) as

$$\begin{aligned}
\bar{f}_{\mathrm{sur}} &= \frac{1}{n-\delta m} \sum_{i=\delta m+1}^{n} E(F_{i:n}) \\
&= \sigma \cdot \frac{1}{n-\delta m} \sum_{i=\delta m+1}^{n} \mu_{i:n} + \bar{f}^t.
\end{aligned} \tag{7.24}$$

In this case, the response to selection is the difference between the mean of the individuals that survive and the mean fitness of the population:

$$\begin{aligned}
s_r &= \frac{1}{n}(n-\delta m)(\bar{f}_{\mathrm{sur}} - \bar{f}) \\
&= \sigma \cdot \frac{1}{n} \sum_{i=\delta m+1}^{n} \mu_{i:n} \\
&= \sigma \cdot I.
\end{aligned} \tag{7.25}$$

Therefore, the selection intensity caused by choosing the worst individuals to be replaced is

$$\begin{aligned}
I_r &= \frac{1}{n}\sum_{i=\delta m+1}^{n} \mu_{i:n} \tag{7.26} \\
&\approx \phi(\Phi^{-1}(1-\delta\rho)). \tag{7.27}
\end{aligned}$$

In this case, the maximum of I_r is $\phi(0) = 1/\sqrt{2\pi} = 0.3989$, which is a fairly low value, but it is not negligible. When the migration policy is to replace individuals randomly in the target deme, there is no differential between the average fitness of the individuals that survive and the average fitness of the entire deme. Therefore, in this case $I_r = 0$.

The overall selection intensity caused by migration is simply

$$I_m = I_e + I_r. \tag{7.28}$$

To predict the convergence time, we should add I_m to the intensity from the selection method used to select the parents of the next generation in each deme (given in Table 7.1). The total intensity is then used in Equation 7.11 to obtain the number of generations until convergence.

3.2   COMPARING THE MIGRATION POLICIES

The simple analysis of the takeover times in Section 2 showed the trends in selection pressure that may be expected from the migration policies. This section confirms the previous observations and provides reference tables for frequently-used configurations of parallel GAs.

Figure 7.2 presents plots of (the approximations of) I_m for topologies with different degrees and varying the migration rate.[4] The maximum migration rate in the case when the best individuals migrate and replace the worst at the target is $\rho^* = 1/(\delta+1)$, where I_m reaches its maximum. At this migration rate, the migrants replace all but the $n/(\delta+1)$ best individuals already present in the deme. In the case when the best migrants replace random individuals, the maximum of I occurs at $\rho = 0.5$, but the highest migration rate that makes sense to use is $\rho^* = 1/\delta$ (for $\delta > 1$), because there are no more than $\delta\rho^*$ individuals in a deme. Finally, when random emigrants replace the worst individuals, the maximum of I_m is at $\rho^* = 1/(2\delta)$. In this case, the average fitness of the migrants is the same as the average fitness of the populations $\bar{f}_{\text{mig}} = \bar{f}$, and as long as the migrants replace the lowest half of the individuals in the receiving deme, the selection differential $s_r = \bar{f}_{\text{sur}} - \bar{f}$ will be positive. Beyond that point, the average fitness of the survivors would decrease.

It is easy to see from the plots that the migration policy with the highest intensity is when the best individuals migrate and replace the worst, followed closely by the case when the best migrants replace random individuals. The difference between these two policies is not as large as the

---

[4]$\Phi^{-1}(x)$ in Equations 7.23 and 7.27 was calculated numerically using Mathematica 3.0 as $\sqrt{2}$InverseErf[0,2x-1]

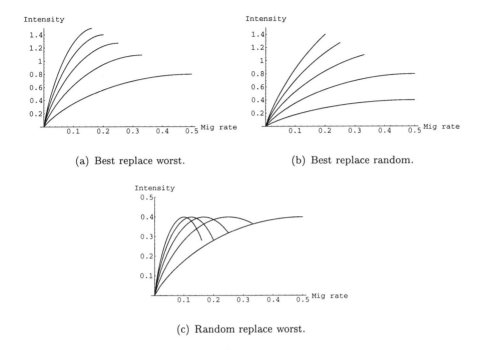

(a) Best replace worst.

(b) Best replace random.

(c) Random replace worst.

Figure 7.2. Selection intensity for different migration policies varying the number of neighbors ($\delta=1,2,..,5$, from bottom to top) and the migration rate.

difference with the policy where migrants are selected randomly, which is consistent with the takeover time calculations.

Tables 7.2, 7.3, and 7.4 have values of I_m for common configurations. Observe that the magnitude of I_m is fairly large. For example, in the case where the best migrants replace the worst individuals, a hypercube of degree $\delta = 3$ and using only 5% migration produces approximately the same selection intensity as tournament selection with $s = 3$ (see Table 7.5). Further comparisons between the tables of I_m and Table 7.5 suggest that migration alone is capable of producing significant selection pressures and can cause the populations to converge fast.

Notice also that when the best individuals migrate, the relation between δ and ρ is not linear. The selection intensity produced by two neighbors using $\rho = 0.05$ is greater than the selection intensity caused by one neighbor sending a fraction $\rho = 0.10$ of its individuals.

As an aside, note that it is possible to reduce the selection pressure with migration. The largest reduction would result from selecting the worst individuals to migrate and replace the best individuals of the receiving deme. Selecting the worst individuals to migrate and replacing

Table 7.2. I_m when the *best* individuals migrate and replace the *worst* individuals at the receiving deme.

ρ	0.01	0.05	0.10	0.15	0.20	0.25	0.30	0.40	0.5
$\delta = 1$	0.053	0.206	0.350	0.466	0.559	0.635	0.695	0.772	0.797
$\delta = 2$	0.101	0.381	0.630	0.814	0.946	1.034	1.081		
$\delta = 3$	0.147	0.542	0.874	1.095	1.226	1.271			
$\delta = 4$	0.192	0.692	1.088	1.318	1.399				
$\delta = 5$	0.236	0.833	1.276	1.483					

Table 7.3. I_m when the *best* individuals migrate and replace *random* individuals at the receiving deme.

ρ	0.01	0.05	0.10	0.15	0.20	0.25	0.30	0.40	0.5
$\delta = 1$	0.026	0.103	0.175	0.233	0.279	0.317	0.347	0.386	0.398
$\delta = 2$	0.053	0.206	0.350	0.466	0.559	0.635	0.695	0.772	0.797
$\delta = 3$	0.079	0.309	0.526	0.699	0.839	0.953	1.043		
$\delta = 4$	0.106	0.412	0.701	0.932	1.119	1.271			
$\delta = 5$	0.133	0.515	0.877	1.165	1.399				

Table 7.4. I_m when *random* individuals migrate and replace the *worst* individuals at the receiving deme.

ρ	0.01	0.05	0.10	0.15	0.20	0.25	0.30	0.40	0.5
$\delta = 1$	0.026	0.103	0.175	0.233	0.279	0.317	0.347	0.386	0.398
$\delta = 2$	0.048	0.175	0.279	0.347	0.386	0.398	0.386		
$\delta = 3$	0.068	0.233	0.347	0.395	0.386	0.317			
$\delta = 4$	0.086	0.279	0.386	0.386	0.279				
$\delta = 5$	0.103	0.317	0.398	0.317					

randomly in the target deme would produce an intermediate reduction of selection pressure. The smallest reduction would be caused by selecting emigrants at random and replacing the best individuals. Calculations similar to those in the previous section would quantify the decrease in selection intensity. Why would we want to reduce the selection intensity with migration? The answer is the same as in a serial GA: to slow down convergence so that the variation operators have enough time to create new solutions. This may be particularly important when low crossover rates are used or when the demes are very small.

Table 7.5. Selection intensity for different tournament sizes ($\mu_{s:s}$)

s	2	3	4	5	6	7	8	16	32
I	0.564	0.846	1.029	1.162	1.267	1.352	1.423	1.766	2.069

4 EXPERIMENTS

This section presents experiments that verify the accuracy of the predictions of the previous section. The experiments use the four migration policies, and the results shown are the average of 20 independent runs for each parameter setting.

All experiments use a 500-bit one-max function, and the populations are initialized randomly (on average $P_0 = 0.5$). Each deme is a generational GA with $n_d = 100$ individuals, which is sufficient to ensure convergence to the optimum in all cases. The GAs use pairwise tournament selection ($s = 2$, $I = 0.5642$), uniform crossover with probability 1.0, and no mutation. The experiments vary the migration rate and the degree of the topology. Migration occurs every generation.

4.1 BEST MIGRANTS REPLACE WORST INDIVIDUALS

The first set of experiments uses Equation 7.10, which predicts the number of bits correct over time, to assess the accuracy of the calculations of I. Figure 7.3 presents the results of experiments using a fully-connected topology with two demes ($\delta = 1$). Note that the accuracy of the predictions decreases slightly as higher migration rates are used. A possible explanation for the small discrepancies is that it is likely that the migrants are different from the individuals already present in a deme (although their average fitness is the same). The increased diversity would require additional mixing (crossover) of alleles to produce a distribution closer to a binomial. The problem is aggravated as longer strings and higher migration rates are used. A similar discrepancy was observed in the 500-bit one-max experiments in Chapter 2. The predictions should be much more accurate for algorithms such as PBIL (Baluja, 1994), UMDA (Mühlenbein & Paaß, 1996), or the compact GA (Harik, Lobo, & Goldberg, 1998) that treat each bit independently, and do not suffer from the inadequate mixing problem described here. However, the predictions are adequate for the purposes of this chapter.

The next set of experiments is designed to verify the prediction of the number of generations until convergence (Equation 7.11). Recall that

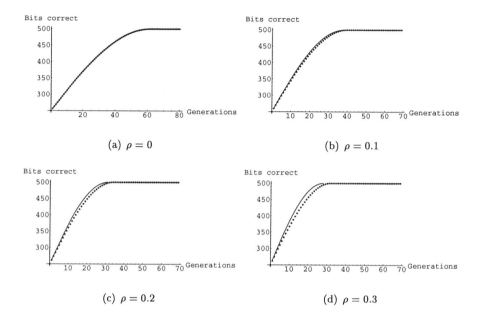

Figure 7.3. Bits correct in a topology with one neighbor using different migration rates. The line is the prediction from Equation 7.10 and the dots are the experimental results.

in this migration policy, both the choices of migrants and replacements increase the selection pressure, and therefore I_m is calculated by adding Equations 7.23 and 7.27. Then, the selection intensity from pairwise tournament selection is added, and the result is used as I in Equation 7.11. The theoretical predictions and the experimental results are presented in Figure 7.4.

Experiments with other topologies of the same degree show no difference. In particular, experiments with 8 demes connected as uni- and bi-directional rings ($\delta = 1$ and 2, respectively) and hypercubes of degree $\delta = 3$ and 4 (16 demes) yield identical results as those with fully-connected topologies in Figures 7.3 and 7.4. For this reason, in the remainder we experiment only with fully-connected topologies.

4.2   BEST MIGRANTS REPLACE RANDOM INDIVIDUALS

For this migration policy, I_e is given by Equation 7.23 and $I_r = 0$. The results are presented in Figure 7.5. We can observe that the convergence is only slightly slower than in the previous case, where the replacements were chosen according to their fitness. This observation supports the

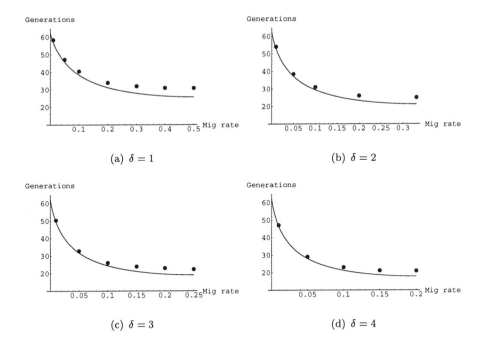

Figure 7.4. Number of generations until convergence when the *best* individuals migrate and replace the *worst*. The line plots the predictions (Equation 7.11) and the dots are the experimental results.

hypothesis raised by the analysis of takeover times that indicated that the selection of emigrants affects the selection pressure more than the selection of replacements.

4.3 RANDOM MIGRANTS REPLACE WORST INDIVIDUALS

In this migration policy, there is no selection pressure caused from selecting random emigrants ($I_e = 0$), but replacing the worst individuals in the target deme causes the intensity to increase. I_r is given by Equation 7.27.

We can observe in Figure 7.6 that since the additional selection pressure caused by this migration policy is not very strong, the generations until convergence do not decrease as much as in the previous cases. We used migration rates higher than the maximum $\rho^* = 1/(2\delta)$ rate that makes sense in this case to be consistent with the previous experiments, and to illustrate how the selection pressure decreases after this point.

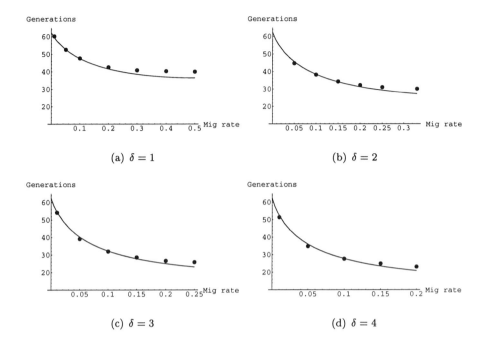

Figure 7.5. Number of generations until convergence when the *best* individuals migrate and replace *random* individuals. The line plots the predictions (Eq. 7.11) and the dots are the experimental results.

5   SUPERLINEAR SPEEDUPS

In the GA community, there has been some controversy about claims of superlinear speedups. The primary reason to suspect these claims is a common argument used to dismiss superlinear speedups in general: if all the tasks of a parallel program are executed by several threads on a single processor, the total execution time cannot be less than the execution time of a serial program that performs the *same* computations. As Punch (1998) points out, the key assumption is that that the serial and parallel programs execute the exact same tasks. In this view, the only possible explanation of superlinear speedups is that the parallel GA somehow executes less work than the serial GA. Unfortunately, the current explanations of the reduction of work are not very satisfactory. While some studies recognize that the choices of migration rates, frequency of migration, choice of migrants and topology have some effect on the amount of work, they fail to ask *why* the work is reduced. This is a very complex question that requires further research, but we examine two possible reasons in this section.

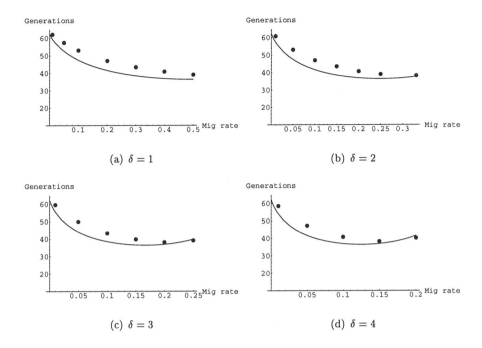

Figure 7.6. Number of generations until convergence when *random* individuals migrate and replace the *worst*. The line plots the predictions (Eq. 7.11) and the dots are the experimental results.

First, it is very likely that multiple populations find different solutions, and therefore migration may introduce to each deme individuals that are different from the native ones. The increased diversity in each deme may have two effects. One is that the increased diversity will delay the convergence of the algorithm. This may give enough time[5] to the crossover operator to mix BBs together into solutions of higher quality than those reachable by a simple GA with an aggregate population (Goldberg, 1998). This means that the demes may be reduced and still reach the same solution as the serial GA, and, in some cases, the reduction may be sufficient to obtain superlinear speedups. The other effect of introducing diverse individuals to a deme is that it may be possible to evolve partial solutions independently in different demes and integrate them after migration. Starkweather et al. (1991) and Whitley et al. (1999) have reported some promising work about this possibil-

---

[5]See the papers by Goldberg, Deb, and Thierens (1993) and Thierens and Goldberg (1993) for a discussion on the time required to mix BBs into good solutions and the relation of this "innovation time" with the success of the search.

ity considering separable functions. This explanation suggests that it is possible to reduce the size of the demes because it is not necessary to solve the entire problem at once.

Another explanation for the reduction of the work in multi-deme GAs is that the migration policy affects the selection pressure. Increasing the selection pressure accelerates the convergence (see Equation 7.11), and this may result in superlinear speedups if the parallel GA is compared (improperly?) against a serial GA with the original—weaker—selection pressure.

To illustrate how the migration policy can affect the speedups of parallel GAs, consider an example with a 500-bit one-max function. A simple GA with a single population of $n = 100$ individuals reached the global solution in all of 20 independent trials (using uniform crossover, pairwise tournament selection, and no mutation). We verified empirically that this population size was the smallest that consistently reached the global optimum. The execution time of the serial GA can be estimated as $T_s = g_s n T_f$, where g_s is the number of generations until convergence and T_f is the function evaluation time. With $l = 500$, $P_0 = 0.5$, and using pairwise tournaments ($I = 0.5642$), Equation 7.11 gives $g_s = 62$. For the purposes of the example, let $T_f = 1$ unit of time, and therefore $T_s = 6200$.

For the parallel case, consider $r = 4$ demes with $n_d = 25$ individuals each, and the same parameters as the serial GA. Suppose that the demes are connected by a bi-directional ring ($\delta = 2$) and use a migration rate of $\rho = 0.05$. We validated empirically that this configuration reaches the optimum in all of 20 independent runs, and that this was the smallest deme size to do so. The execution time in the parallel case is $T_p = g_p n_d T_f + T_c$, where T_c is the total time used in communications. T_c depends on δ and ρ, and for our example we will set it to a large value: $T_c = 100.$[6] The value of $I_m = 0.381$ may be found in Table 7.2. Substituting $I = 0.5642 + 0.381$ in Equation 7.11 gives $g_p = 37$. With these values, $T_p = 1025$, and the ratio $\frac{T_s}{T_p} = 6.05$, which, even with the conservative values used here, is considerably higher than the ideal speedup of 4.

This explanation of superlinear speedups is consistent with many experimental results. For example, Koza and Andre (1995) and Andre and Koza (1998) report superlinear speedups on genetic programming applications that use the same total population size and reach the same

---

[6]Notice that the ratio of T_c/T_f is extremely high. In most practical applications of parallel GAs this ratio is much lower than one. We are being overly conservative here.

solution quality in serial and parallel. In both cases, the migrants were chosen probabilistically according to their fitness.

We can argue that since the multi-deme GA has a higher selection pressure and executes less work, it is a different algorithm than the single-population GA. Perhaps a more fair comparison would be between algorithms with the same selection intensity, but as we shall see in the next section, having the same intensity does not mean that the algorithms are equivalent.

We should not conclude that all claims of superlinear speedups are caused by an increase of selection pressure due to migration. Other possible causes are implementation particulars (for example, the smaller demes may fit completely in the processors' caches, reducing the memory access times enough to produce superlinear speedups (Belding, 1995); or inappropriate sizing of populations, such that convergence to solutions of the same quality is not guaranteed). Another possible cause of superlinear speedups is to use the parallel code to obtain timings for the serial case, because this may artificially inflate the serial execution time with unnecessary operations.

6 VARIANCE AND THE HIGHER CUMULANTS

The analysis of the selection intensity considers only the changes in the mean fitness of the population, but we can extend it easily to study the effects of migration on the variance and the higher cumulants of the distribution of fitness (Cantú-Paz, 2000b). The cumulants of a distribution are related to the central moments. The r-th central moment of the distribution of fitness of a population of size n is

$$\mu_r = \frac{1}{n} \sum_{i=1}^{n} (f_i - \bar{f})^r, \tag{7.29}$$

where f_i is the fitness of the i-th individual, and $\bar{f} = \frac{1}{n} \sum_{i=1}^{n} f_i$ is the mean fitness. The first three cumulants are equal to the first central moments. The fourth cumulant is $\kappa_4 = \mu_4 - 3\mu_2^2$.

The first cumulant is the mean ($\kappa_1 = \mu_1 = \bar{f}$), and the second is the variance ($\kappa_2 = \mu_2 = \sigma_f^2$). The third and fourth cumulants give additional information about the shape of the distribution, and sometimes they are divided by $\kappa_2^{r/2}$ to obtain the skewness and kurtosis coefficients. The skewness measures the asymmetry of the distribution; it is negative if a distribution is skewed to the left, and it is positive if the distribution is skewed to the right. The kurtosis measures the "peakedness" of the distribution; a negative kurtosis indicates that the distribution is flatter

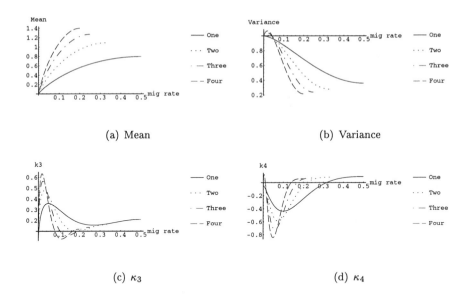

(a) Mean (b) Variance

(c) κ_3 (d) κ_4

Figure 7.7. The first four cumulants of the fitness distribution varying the migration rate and the number of neighbors.

than a normal, and a positive kurtosis indicates that the distribution is more peaked than a normal.

We restrict our attention to the case when the best individuals are selected to migrate and replace the worst individuals in the receiving deme. The r-th moment of the fitness distribution after migration has two components that correspond to the migrants and to the native individuals that are not replaced at the receiving deme:

$$\mu_r^{\text{mig}} = \frac{\delta}{n} \sum_{i=n-n\rho+1}^{n} (\mu_{i:n} - \bar{Z}^{\text{mig}})^r + $$
$$\frac{1}{n} \sum_{i=\delta\rho n+1}^{n} (\mu_{i:n} - \bar{Z}^{\text{mig}})^r. \tag{7.30}$$

Figure 7.7 shows plots of the first four cumulants of the distribution of fitness varying the migration rate and the number of neighbors. Figure 7.7a is the same as Figure 7.2a. The original population (before migration) had a standard normal distribution ($\kappa_1 = \kappa_3 = \kappa_4 = 0, \kappa_2 = 1$). Note that in configurations with more than one neighbor and low migration rates, the variance is higher than the original value of one. This seems to occur at approximately $\rho = 0.02$ or 0.03, regardless of the number of neighbors.

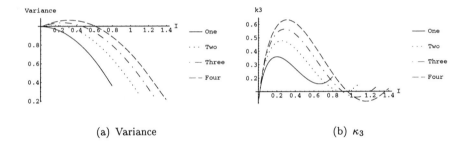

Figure 7.8. The second and third cumulants of the fitness distribution in configurations with the same selection intensity.

Figure 7.8 plots the variance and the third cumulant of the fitness distribution against the selection intensity. This graph clearly shows that different configurations, even if they have the same selection intensity, affect the distribution in different ways. A deme with more neighbors has a higher fitness variance after migration, as well as a higher skewness.

The fitness variance is an indicator of diversity. Preserving (or increasing) the diversity in a deme is desirable for at least two reasons. The first is that the increased diversity will delay the convergence of the algorithm, which as we discussed earlier, may give enough time to the crossover operator to mix BBs together into solutions of high quality. The other effect of preserving diversity in a deme is that it may be possible to evolve partial solutions independently in different demes and integrate them after migration.

7 SUMMARY

The choice of migrants and the replacement of individuals are not often considered important parameters of parallel GAs. However, this chapter used two different methods to show that choosing the migrants or replacements according to their fitness increases the selection pressure. Some migration policies may cause the algorithm to converge significantly faster. The migration policy that accelerates convergence the most is to choose both the migrants and the replacements according to their fitness, which is also the most common policy.

The faster convergence may explain some of the claims of superlinear speedups in parallel GAs. This chapter showed an example where serial and parallel algorithms reached the same solution and used the same number of individuals, but the additional selection pressure resulted in superlinear speedups.

The chapter also included calculations of the higher moments of the distribution of fitness. These calculations showed that different combinations of the degree of the topology and the migration rate affect the population in different ways, even if they result in the same selection intensity.

Chapter 8

FINE-GRAINED AND HIERARCHICAL PARALLEL GENETIC ALGORITHMS

Earlier chapters of this book showed how to optimize master-slave and multiple-deme parallel GAs. At this point, we face a critical question: given a problem and a parallel computer, what algorithm returns the desired solution in the shortest time? A valid answer would be to find the optimal configurations of the two algorithms and choose the fastest one. However, the choice of algorithms is complicated further because there are other options: we could use a fine-grained parallel GA, or we may combine multiple demes with other parallel GAs to form hierarchical algorithms, which have potentially better performance than either of their components.

Traditionally, fine-grained GAs have not received as much attention as the other types of parallel GAs, and consequently there are not many results to guide their design. This chapter describes the algorithms, some of their design problems, and the available results. However, the focus of the chapter is on the hierarchical algorithms, and specifically on combinations of multiple-deme and master-slave algorithms. As before, our interest is to find the desired solution in the shortest time possible. The configuration of the hierarchical algorithms is easy to optimize if there are enough processors available. However, when the supply of processors is limited, they have to be allocated carefully between demes and slaves to obtain the fastest hierarchical GA possible. That is the main goal of this chapter. It presents a method that integrates previous results to determine the optimal combination of demes and slaves.

The chapter begins with a description of fine-grained GAs and a brief review of previous work. Then, different types of hierarchical GAs are examined in Section 2. Section 3 discusses how to design optimal hierarchical GAs and Section 4 gives a complete example that illustrates how to use the theory on a particular problem and hardware environment. The chapter ends with a summary in Section 5.

1   FINE-GRAINED PARALLEL GAs

A fine-grained GA consists on one population distributed on a mesh that limits the interactions between individuals: selection and recombination occur only within neighborhoods defined by the structure of the mesh (Manderick & Spiessens, 1989). Most frequently, the mesh is a simple two-dimensional rectangular grid (see Figure 1.3), but other structures are possible. The neighborhoods overlap and good solutions may disseminate across the entire population. Fine-grained GAs are also known as diffusion GAs (Pettey, 1997), cellular GAs (Whitley, 1993a; Tomassini, 1993), or massively-parallel GAs (Baluja, 1992).

As in the other GAs, we need to determine the size of the population, and the parameters that control selection, crossover, and mutation. In addition, this type of parallel GAs has its own set of parameters: the topology of the mesh; the size and shape of the neighborhoods; the methods use to select, mate, and replace individuals; and the distribution of the population structure to multiple processors. This section reviews some of the previous work that identified and tried to answer some of the important questions in the design of fine-grained parallel GAs.

Some of the first fine-grained parallel GAs are traditional simple GAs implemented on massively parallel computers. Robertson (1987) described an early fine-grained GA on a Connection Machine 1. This algorithm was intended as a component of a genetic classifier system, and therefore it selected and replaced only a small fraction of the population on each generation. Robertson parallelized all the components of the algorithm: the selection of parents, the selection of classifiers to replace, crossover, and mutation. He reported that the algorithm was very efficient, and that its execution time was independent of the population size (up to 16K, which was the number of processing elements in the CM-1), which allowed the users to experiment with much larger populations than was common. Global selection is the bottleneck in efficient fine-grained implementations of GAs, but Branke, Andersen, and Schmeck (1996) presented and compared four efficient global selection algorithms that operate on a 2-D mesh. Their analysis showed that the execution time of all of their algorithms was $O(\sqrt{N})$ on a $N \times N$ mesh.

Manderick and Spiessens (1989) recognized that GAs could be adapted easily to massively parallel computers by eliminating the global selection and random mating. They realized that the behavior of the new algorithm would not be identical to the simple GA, and identified the population's and neighborhood's sizes as important parameters of the algorithm. Manderick and Spiessens also noticed that these algorithms are better simulations of the local selection and mating that occur in natural populations.

Working independently, Gorges-Schleuter (1989a, 1989b) and Mühlenbein (1989a, 1989b) introduced ASPARAGOS. ASPARAGOS is an asynchronous fine-grained parallel GA that used a population structure that resembles a ladder with the upper and lower ends tied together. ASPARAGOS was used to solve some difficult combinatorial optimization problems with great success. Later, different population structures (Gorges-Schleuter, 1991) and mating strategies were compared (Gorges-Schleuter, 1992). ASPARAGOS uses a local hillclimbing algorithm to try to improve the fitness of the individuals in its population. This makes it difficult to isolate the contribution of the spatial structure of the population to the search quality. However, ASPARAGOS is a very effective optimization tool.

There have been significant advancements in the analysis of some aspects of these algorithms. In particular, the size of the neighborhood has received considerable attention. Early on, Manderick and Spiessens (1989) observed that the performance (solution quality) of the algorithm degraded as the size of the neighborhood increased, and suggested to use moderately-sized neighborhoods. Spiessens and Manderick (1991) showed that for a neighborhood size s and a string length l, the execution time of the algorithm was $O(s+l)$ or $O(s(\log s)+l)$ time steps, depending on the selection scheme used.

More recently, Sarma and De Jong (1996, 1997) determined that varying the size and the shape of the neighborhoods affects the selection pressure. They found that the ratio of the radius of the neighborhood to the radius of the entire population is a critical parameter that determines the selection pressure. Their analysis quantified the time to spread a single good solution across the entire population using different neighborhood sizes, in a manner analogous to the takeover time of tournament selection in simple GAs. This is an important result that can explain many observations reported in the literature. Later, they extended the analysis to consider dynamic environments (Sarma & De Jong, 1999), and observed that fine-grained GAs seem to perform better than simple GAs without requiring modifications (although some modifications help, see Kirley (2000)). Others have extended Sarma and De Jong's basic model to consider different mating strategies and population structures (Gorges-Schleuter, 1999).

Rudolph (2000a) investigated takeover times in spatially-distributed populations. He calculated lower bounds of the takeover time for arbitrary structures, lower and upper bounds for grid-like structures, and an exact expression for rings. The lower bound of the takeover time is the diameter of the graph (i.e., the largest number of edges that separate any two vertices in the graph). This suggests that population structures with short diameters have a stronger selection pressure, which is consistent with the early empirical observations of Gorges-Schleuter (1991) and with De Jong and Sarma's models. Rudolph conjectured that the takeover time depends more strongly on the diameter of the graph than on the particular selection method used.

An area open for future research is to calculate the selection intensity of different selection schemes used in fine-grained parallel EAs. Although there is a good understanding of the takeover times, calculations of the selection intensity are still nonexistent. These calculations would permit us to compare very accurately the selection pressure across different models of parallel EAs.

Choosing a topology is another important question in fine-grained parallel GAs, and it has been studied empirically several times. Anderson and Ferris (1990) tried different population structures and replacement algorithms. They experimented with two rings, a hypercube, two meshes and an "island" structure where only one individual of each deme overlapped with other demes. They concluded that, for the particular problem they were trying to solve (balancing an assembly line), the ring and the "island" structures were the best choices.

Baluja (1992, 1993) compared a 2-D mesh with two variations of a linear structure, and found that the mesh gave the best results on almost all the problems tested. Schwehm (1992) reported similar results. He compared a ring, a torus, a $16 \times 8 \times 8$ cube, a $4 \times 4 \times 4 \times 4 \times 4$ hypercube, and a 10-D hypercube. The algorithm with the torus structure converged faster than the other algorithms, but there was no mention of the solution quality. Shapiro and Navetta (1994) used a fine-grained GA algorithm to predict the secondary structure of RNA. They tried different logical topologies: all eight nearest neighbors, four nearest neighbors, and all neighbors within a specified distance d. The results for $d > 2$ were the poorest, and the four-neighbor scheme consistently outperformed the topology with eight neighbors.

Of course, fine-grained parallel GAs have been used to solve some difficult application problems. For example, two-dimensional bin packing is a popular benchmark problem, and Kröger et al. (1991, 1992, 1993) found satisfactory solutions. Tamaki and Nishikawa (1992) successfully applied fine-grained GAs to the job shop scheduling problem, and Prabhu (1996) solved image interpretation problems.

A few papers compare fine- and coarse-grained parallel GAs (Baluja, 1993; Gordon & Whitley, 1993). In these comparisons, sometimes fine-grained GAs come ahead of the coarse-grained GAs, but sometimes it is just the opposite, depending on the criteria used to compare the algorithms. Manderick and Spiessens (1989) conjectured that fine-grained algorithms have an advantage on multi-modal problems, and further observations by Collins and Jefferson (1991) and Gorges-Schleuter (1991) suggest that this may be the case.

Gordon, Whitley, and Böhm (1992) showed that the critical path of a fine-grained algorithm is shorter than that of a multiple-population GA. This suggests that if enough processors were available, massively parallel GAs would need less time to finish their execution, regardless of the population size. Although this was a theoretical study that did not include considerations such as the communications bandwidth or memory requirements, it is consistent with the early empirical reports of Manderick and Spiessens (1989). Gordon (1994) studied the spatial locality of memory references in different models of parallel GAs. This analysis is useful in determining the most adequate computing platform for each model.

Sprave (1999) presented a unified view of fine-grained and island population structures using hypergraphs (a generalization of graphs where an edge can represent relations between arbitrary subsets of vertices). The model can represent arbitrary topologies, migration policies, and migration intervals. It is "intended as a base for further theoretical work in the field of non-panmictic population structures", and Sprave demonstrated the model's utility to calculate takeover times.

Like the island model, the fine-grained model has interesting algorithmic properties, regardless of its implementation on serial or parallel computers. It provides a natural way to isolate groups of similar individuals that, for instance, may be beneficial to solve multimodal optimization problems. In some cases, it is desirable to identify multiple promising solutions so that the user can decide between them. Fortunately, it is very easy to extend these algorithms with a niching technique so they can stably maintain multiple optima in the population, as Manderick and Spiessens (1989) recognized. In addition, Kirley and Green (2000) showed how simple extensions to the algorithm can address multi-objective problems very effectively.

One possible reason why fine-grained GAs have not received much attention may be the perception that they require special hardware, such as a Connection Machine (Hillis, 1985) or a cellular automata machine (Toffoli & Margolus, 1987). Certainly, these type of algorithms can be implemented easily and efficiently on massively parallel hardware, but it is also possible to implement them on more readily-accessible parallel hardware or even on serial processors. In fact, Manderick and Spiessens (1989) used a serial simulator to obtain the results of their seminal paper.

If the population is arranged on a 2-D grid, the population may be decomposed into strips or into boxes. Each strip or box can then be assigned to a separate processor. Hart (1994) identified these two options and presented the conditions when one method would be more efficient than the other. Hart et al. (1996) examined the effect of communications between strips or blocks in the number of function evaluations that the algorithm needs to converge. They observed that if communications are asynchronous or if synchronization occurs infrequently, the algorithm needs fewer function evaluations. This reduction is independent of the benefits from the better utilization of processors that is possible with fewer synchronizations.

The fine-grained approach can be used on other evolutionary algorithms, not just GAs. For example, Sprave (1994) and Gorges-Schleuter (1998, 1999) implemented fine-grained evolution strategies and studied the effects of different selection schemes. A notable algorithm that is related to fine-grained parallel GAs is cellular programming (Sipper, 1997). The objective of cellular programming is to use genetic operations to find the rules for each cell of a non-uniform cellular automata (each cell has different rules). Each cell is represented by an individual of the GA, and interactions between individuals are limited to their neighborhoods, just as in fine-grained GAs. Several applications are described by Capcarrère et al. (1999), who also proposed some statistics that can be used to study the dynamics of cellular algorithms.

Fine-grained parallel GAs seem very promising, and there are multiple opportunities to expand them in many directions. The next chapter will outline some possible research directions, but first, the next section will show how to use fine-grained and other algorithms in hierarchical configurations.

2   HIERARCHICAL PARALLEL GAs

Previous chapters have shown that both master-slave and multiple-deme parallel GAs can quickly reach good solutions when they are designed properly, but even greater improvements are possible by combining two basic forms of parallel GA into a hierarchical algorithm. Grefenstette (1981) was the first to propose this. The fundamental idea is simple: use a multiple-deme algorithm where the demes themselves are some form of parallel GAs. At the higher level, the algorithm may be designed with the theory presented in previous chapters. At the lower level, there are three choices: use a fine-grained GA, use a master-slave GA, or use a multiple-deme GA with very high migration to give the illusion of

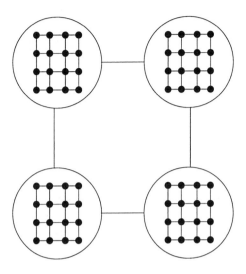

Figure 8.1. This hierarchical GA combines a multi-deme GA (at the upper level) and a fine-grained GA (at the lower level).

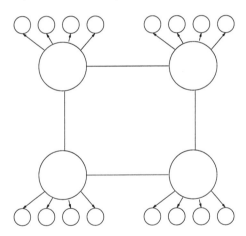

Figure 8.2. At the upper level this hybrid is a multi-deme parallel GA where each node is a master-slave GA.

a single population. The remainder of this section examines the three types of hierarchical parallel GAs.

Figure 8.1 presents a schematic of hierarchical GA with a fine-grained GA at the lower level. This algorithm was proposed by Manderick and Spiessens (1989) as an extension to the conventional fine-grained algorithms that they examined. An example of this type of hybrid is the "mixed" parallel GA invented by Gruau (1994). In his algorithm, the

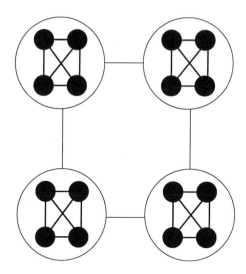

Figure 8.3. This hybrid uses multi-deme GAs at both the upper and the lower levels. At the lower level intense migration gives the illusion of a single panmictic population.

population of each deme was placed on a 2-D grid, and the demes were connected as a 2-D torus. Migration between demes occurred at regular intervals, and Gruau reported good results for a original neural network design and training application.

Another hybrid with a fine-grained GA at the lower level is Asparagos96 (Gorges-Schleuter, 1997). It was proposed as an extension to ASPARAGOS, one of the first fine-grained GAs. The hybrid used a ring topology to connect the demes, and the structure of the demes was also a ring. The migration rate varied over time: it was very low at the start of the run, and it increased linearly—and very slowly—as a function of the generation number. In effect, migration is not expected to occur until the run is very advanced, somewhat similar to the migration strategy used by the multiple-deme GAs in Chapters 4 to 6. After all the populations converged, Asparagos96 used the best and second best individuals of each deme as the initial population of a simple GA to try to refine the solutions further.

Lin, Goodman, and Punch III (1997) also used a multi-population GA with spatially-structured subpopulations. They also used a ring topology to connect the subpopulations, but each deme was structured as a torus. The authors compared their hybrid against a simple GA, a fine-grained GA, two multiple-population GAs with a ring topology (one used 5 demes and variable deme sizes, the other used a constant deme size of 50 individuals and different number of demes), and another multi-deme

GA with demes connected on a torus. Migration occurred at regular intervals; the best individuals of each deme were selected as migrants, and they replaced the worst individuals at the receiving deme. Chapter 7 argued that this migration scheme increases the selection pressure, and that convergence occurs faster than in a simple population. The experimental design was similar to Tanese's where the total number of individuals is fixed, and were distributed to processors in different ways. Using a job shop scheduling problem as a benchmark, they reported that the simple GA found inferior solutions to all the other methods, and that increasing the number of demes had a larger positive effect on the solution quality than increasing the sizes of the demes or the total population size.

Another type of hierarchical parallel GA uses a master-slave on each of the demes of a multi-population GA (see Figure 8.2 for a schematic). Migration occurs as usual, and the evaluation of the individuals is handled in parallel by the slaves. This approach does not introduce any new analytic problems, and it will be examined in detail in the next section. Bianchini and Brown (1993) presented an example of this algorithm, and showed that it can find a solution of the same quality of a master-slave parallel GA or a multi-deme GA in less time.

A very similar concept was invented by Goldberg (1989a) in the context of an object-oriented implementation of a "community model" parallel GA. In each "community" (think deme) there are multiple houses (slaves) where parents reproduce and the offspring are evaluated. In the algorithm, there are multiple communities, and it is possible that individuals migrate to other places.

The third method of hybridizing parallel GAs is to use multi-deme GAs at both the upper and lower levels (see Figure 8.3). The idea is to force panmictic mixing at the lower level by using a high migration rate and a dense topology, while a low migration rate is used at the high level (Goldberg, 1996a). We may use an algorithm similar to the GA with the distributed panmictic population presented in Chapter 3. Analytically, this hybrid would be equivalent to a multiple-population GA if the panmictic groups are considered as a single deme. This method has not been implemented yet.

3   OPTIMAL HIERARCHICAL PARALLEL GAs

This section presents a method to design an optimal hierarchical parallel GA with master-slave GAs at the lower level. Properly-designed hierarchical implementations should reduce the execution time more than either of their components. In particular, the execution time of each of the upper-level demes is reduced by a factor equal to the speedup at the lower level. Therefore, the overall speedup is given by $Sp_{md} \times Sp_{ms}$, where Sp_{md} is the speedup that originates from dividing the population into multiple demes, and Sp_{ms} is the speedup from evaluating the demes using multiple slaves.

The ideal situation would be to use the optimal number of demes, r^*, and the optimal number of slaves, S^*. However, the number of processors available ($\mathcal{P}$) may be less than the processors required to use r^* and S^*: $r^* \times (S^* + 1)$. If that is the case, then the processors should be allocated between demes and slaves to maximize the overall speedup. One alternative to find the optimal configuration is simply to enumerate all possible pairs, calculate the expected speedup for each, and choose the pair with the highest speedup. Although the calculations are inexpensive and the number of valid demes-slaves pairs is not too large, in fact not all of the possible pairs need to be considered.

The key to design optimal hierarchical parallel GAs is to design the upper level first and then the lower level. At the upper level, the number of demes may vary from one to the number of processors available, and since the best number of demes is unknown, this step involves enumerating all the $\mathcal{P}$ possibilities. For each deme count, the connectivity of the topology may be optimized using the models of Chapter 6. The result is an optimal degree that can be used directly to calculate the optimal deme size using Equation 6.12.

Once the deme size is known, designing the lower level of the hierarchical GA is straightforward. The design consists on finding the optimal number of slaves for each deme count. Recall that the optimal number of processors in a master-slave GA is $\sqrt{n\gamma}$. In this case, n corresponds to the deme size. It may turn out that the optimal number of slaves is too large, and that there are not enough processors available ($S^* \times r > \mathcal{P}$). In this case, the number of slaves that should be used is the largest possible, $\lfloor \mathcal{P}/r \rfloor$. Since for every deme count there is one optimal number of slaves, the number of candidate configurations that need to be evaluated is equal to the number of processors available, $\mathcal{P}$.

This method accounts the two basic forms of parallel GAs: the pure master-slave is accounted for when the number of demes is one, and pure multiple-demes when $r = \mathcal{P}$. No special calculations are required to handle these cases.

Figure 8.4 shows the speedups of the optimal configurations of hierarchical GAs at all possible deme counts. The example considers a situation where there are 1000 processors available, and the three plots correspond to different values of γ (10,100,1000).

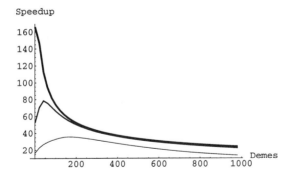

Figure 8.4. Speedups of optimally-configured hybrids of multi-deme and master-slave parallel GAs for $\gamma = T_f/T_c$ ratios of 10, 100 and 1000 (from bottom to top, respectively).

When γ is high, the master-slave GA is capable of almost linear speedups, and configurations with many slaves per deme would probably perform better than many demes with few slaves. Similarly, when communications are relatively expensive, the multiple-deme GAs have an advantage because they communicate infrequently. In this case, higher speedups are obtained using many demes and few (if any) slaves.

4   AN EXAMPLE OF OPTIMAL DESIGN

This section presents an example that illustrates how to use the models introduced in this book to obtain a desired solution in the minimum time. The test function of the example is formed by concatenating ten copies of an 8-bit fully-deceptive function. This is the same test function that was used in the early chapters of the book to validate the models for the bounding cases of multiple-deme GAs. The objective is to reach a solution with eight BBs ($\hat{Q} = 0.8$) in the shortest time.

To make this case study as realistically as possible, we shall use no a priori knowledge about the function. However, to facilitate comparisons with the results of other chapters, the quality of the solutions is measured as the number of partitions that converge to the correct BB.

The first step in this example is to find the hardware-dependent constants. Then, we use the master-slave and multiple-deme models together to enumerate the candidate configurations and find the best, as the previous section described. Finally, we present experiments that verify that the chosen configuration is indeed the best.

4.1   THE HARDWARE

The computer used in this example is an IBM SP-2 with eight processing elements. Each processing element is a Power PC 604 running at 133 Mhz with 256 Mb of memory. The nodes are connected with an IBM High Performance Switch (100 Mbits/sec) and by a 10 Mbits/sec Ethernet. The parallel GA code was programmed in C++ and compiled with IBM's xlC compiler using the -02 flag to optimize the code. Communications were handled by PVM 3.4, and only the fast switch was used in the experiments.

Since the original function is very inexpensive, its execution time was artificially raised to $T_f = 1$ ms. The communication time was measured varying the size of the packets, and for the message lengths that are likely to be used in this example the time was approximately 1 ms.

4.2   FINDING THE BEST CONFIGURATION

The first step to use the theory is to calibrate the gambler's ruin model to the particular problem. A simple GA with pairwise tournament selection and one-point crossover was used to experiment. Three runs were performed with population sizes of 100, 200, and 400 individuals. The GA found solutions with 1, 2 and 4 correct BBs, respectively, which is far below the desired 8 BBs and indicates that much larger populations are needed.

The gambler's ruin model has two problem-dependent parameters: the order of the BBs, k, and the correct decision-making probability, p. For a given problem, however, we may group the domain-dependent components into one constant, and use the experimental results to determine its value. Specifically, the gambler's ruin problem may rewritten in the following way:

$$P_{bb} \approx 1 - \left(\frac{1-p}{p}\right)^{n/2^k} = 1 - y^n.$$

A least-squares steepest-descent method was used to fit $Q = 1 - y^n$ to the experimental data.[1] The result is that $y = 0.998786$, which is not very different from the value that would be obtained using the known theoretical values of $p = 0.5334$ and $k = 8$ for this problem ($y = 0.999022$).

---

[1]Specifically, Mathematica 3.0's NonlinearRegress function was used as follows:
data={{100,0.1},{200,0.2},{400,0.4}};
NonlinearRegress[data,1-y^n, n, y, Method->FindMinimum].

Table 8.1.   Optimal configurations for each possible deme count.

r	δ^*	n_d^*	$\mathcal{P}^*$	Slaves used
1	0	1325	36	7
2	1	519	23	3
3	2	405	20	1
4	3	345	19	1
5	4	307	18	0
6	5	279	17	0
7	6	258	16	0
8	7	241	16	0

The population size that a simple GA requires to find 8 BBs may now be easily determined as

$$n = \frac{\ln(1 - \frac{\hat{Q}}{m})}{\ln y} = \frac{\ln(1 - 0.8)}{\ln 0.998786} = 1325,$$

which is consistent with the results obtained in Chapter 2. Since $T_f = T_c = $ 1ms, the optimal number of processors of a master-slave parallel GA on this problem is $\sqrt{1325} = 36$, which is much greater than the eight processors available. Therefore, it is likely that very satisfactory near-linear speedups would be observed if only a simple master-slave GA is used. However, we follow the procedure outlined in the previous section to determine the optimal allocation of processors between demes and slaves.

For each deme count from one to eight, the optimal degree δ^* was computed using Equation 6.14. In all cases, the optimal degree was larger than eight, and therefore the largest degree possible $(r - 1)$ was used in each case.

The optimal degree $(r - 1)$ was used to calculate the optimal deme size using Equation 6.12. Then, using the optimal deme size, the optimal number of processors for a master-slave GA was calculated. The results are presented in Table 8.1. For all deme counts, the optimal number of slaves exceeds the number of processors available, so the maximum possible number of slaves is used.

Experiments were performed with a hierarchical parallel GA using the configurations in Table 8.1. The elapsed time was measured and averaged over ten trials. Each deme used pairwise tournament selection, one-point crossover with probability 1, and no mutation. The hierarchical GA found solutions with at least 8 BBs in all cases, except when $r = 2$ where the average solution had 7.7 BBs. The average speedup

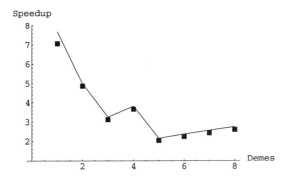

Figure 8.5. Theoretical predictions (line) and experimental results (dots) of the speedups of optimally-configured hybrids of multi-deme and master-slave parallel GAs.

is presented in Figure 8.5 along with the theoretical predictions. The experiments match the theory very well, and confirm that the best configuration for this problem has one deme and seven slaves.

It is interesting to note that if there were more processors available, the optimal configuration would be different. For example, if there were 1000 processors, the optimal configuration would have 166 demes with 6 slaves per deme.

5   SUMMARY

This chapter treated fine-grained and hierarchical parallel GAs. It began with a brief review of fine-grained parallel GAs. The chapter identified some of the most salient design problems of this type of algorithms, and discussed some of the recent work on this area.

This chapter focused on hierarchical combinations of parallel GAs. The hierarchical algorithms are composed of multiple demes, and the demes themselves are parallel GAs. We identified three hierarchical algorithms, and we examined in closer detail one where the upper-level demes are master-slave GAs.

As before, we are interested in obtaining a solution in the shortest time possible, and this chapter introduced a method to distribute the available processors between upper-level demes and lower-level slaves to minimize the execution time. Finally, Section 4 presented a step-by-step example of the use of the theory of this book to a particular problem. The example assumed minimal knowledge about the problem, and showed how only simple experiments are necessary to calibrate the theory to obtain very accurate results.

Chapter 9

SUMMARY, EXTENSIONS, AND CONCLUSIONS

This chapter first summarizes the findings and the recommendations that originate from the research contained in this book. Next, it discusses possible extensions, and finally it presents the conclusions of this study.

1   SUMMARY

The design of efficient and accurate parallel GAs is a complex problem. One must decide on a configuration among the many choices of topologies, migration rates, deme counts and sizes. Each parameter affects the quality of the search and the efficiency of the algorithm in non-linear ways, which makes the choices difficult. The ultimate goal is to determine the configuration that reaches a solution of the required quality as fast as possible. This book made some contributions towards this goal, and are summarized in this section.

The first part of this book considered GAs with one population, and reports two main results. The first is an accurate model of simple GA performance based on the gambler's ruin problem. This model integrates previous knowledge of BB supply and correct decision making into an accurate predictor of solution quality. Chapter 2 presented empirical evidence that validates the accuracy of the predictions on various settings of practical interest. The model was successfully tested with functions of varying difficulty, with noisy fitness functions, and with different levels of selection pressure.

The second contribution is a lower bound on the benefits that should be expected from parallel GAs. The analysis of the simple master-slave GA in Chapter 3 showed that there is an optimal number of processors $\mathcal{P}^* = \sqrt{\frac{nT_f}{T_c}}$ that minimizes the execution time, and that the maximum parallel speedup is $0.5\mathcal{P}^*$. The critical number of processors that maintain a desired efficiency was calculated, and it was used to determine that $\mathcal{P}_l = (\frac{nT_f}{T_c})^{1/3}$ processors maintain a near-perfect efficiency of $1 - \frac{1}{\mathcal{P}_l}$. More sophisticated parallel GAs should be more efficient and produce higher speedups or be discarded.

In addition, Chapter 3 described a parallel implementation of a single-population GA that resembles a bounding case of multiple-deme GAs. Although this algorithm is less efficient than the simple master-slave, it has important theoretical implications. Straightforward calculations show that it can use $O(\sqrt{\frac{nT_f}{T_c}})$ processors to reduce the execution time, which is asymptotically the same number of processors that optimally-configured master-slaves can use.

Most of the book focused on parallel GAs with multiple populations. These algorithms have been very popular, but the effects of their parameters on the solution quality and algorithmic efficiency are not well understood. To begin making progress in the study of multi-deme GAs, Chapter 4 extended the gambler's ruin model to calculate the expected quality of the best of r isolated or fully-connected demes. This chapter shows that distributing the population to multiple demes has two effects on the quality. The first is that the quality required of each deme may be reduced, because in a successful run only one of the demes has to reach the desired solution. The reduction in the target quality translates into smaller demes, which in turn represent a shorter execution time. However, the reduction is only marginal. The second effect of using multiple demes has a greater impact on the quality and occurs when the populations communicate. After migration, the demes restart with more copies of BBs than when they are initialized randomly, and therefore are expected to reach solutions of higher quality.

One key idea introduced in Chapter 4 is to calculate how many copies of the correct BBs are present in the demes after migration. Then, the gambler's ruin model is used to predict the outcome of the second epoch. The same idea is at the core of the more refined models in the remainder of the book.

The calculations in Chapter 4 showed that the isolated bounding case does not result in significant performance improvements, and should be avoided in practice. On the other extreme, the size of the fully-connected demes decreases substantially, thereby reducing considerably the time used by computations. However, the reduction in computations is paired with a rapidly increasing cost of communications. This tradeoff was used to find the deme size and deme count that together minimize the execution time.

Chapter 5 used Markov chains to extend the models of solution quality to consider multiple epochs. The first result of the modeling is that the major improvements in quality come after the second epoch, confirming that the results from the previous chapter are relevant and useful. This chapter also showed that the long-term search quality of r fully-connected demes of size n_d is equivalent to a single GA with a population of size rn_d, when the migration rate is maximal. As the migration rate decreases, the quality deteriorates, but even moderate migration rates are sufficient to reach the same quality as a panmictic population. In any case, since the cost is independent of the migration rate (because migrations occur after convergence), there is no reason to avoid the highest values.

Chapter 5 also introduced the first model of arbitrary topologies. The model explicitly accounts for all the possible combinations of success and failure of the r demes, and therefore it is very accurate, but it is also impractical for large r. Nevertheless, the model showed that the influence of the topology on the solution quality is significant and should be examined further.

Chapter 6 continues the study of the topology. It presented simple approximate models that relate the deme size, the migration rate, and the degree of the topology with the quality and cost of the search. The models explain why demes with many neighbors are more likely to find the desired solution than sparsely-connected demes. The usual tradeoff between decreasing computations and increasing communications appears, and the analysis showed how to choose the degree of the topology that minimizes the total cost.

An important observation made in Chapter 6 is that the optimal degree, δ^*, does not vary considerably as the number of demes is increased. Since the execution time largely depends on the degree, this observation implies that the execution times of optimally-configured topologies do not vary much either. Therefore, *any* optimally-configured topology would be a good choice to reduce the execution time. Previously, the fully-connected topology was optimized, and the results of Chapter 6 suggest that it may be an adequate choice, even though it cannot connect many demes. In fact, an optimal fully-connected topology uses fewer demes ($r^* = \delta^* + 1$) than any other optimally-configured topology, and therefore it is very efficient (in terms of $\frac{Sp}{P}$).

This chapter also established that when the topology is fixed and the algorithm is executed until all the demes converge to the same solution, the optimal number of populations is $O(\sqrt{\frac{nT_f}{T_c}})$, which asymptotically is the same as parallel versions of GAs with a single population. This result suggests that parallel GAs—regardless of whether they use a single or multiple populations—can integrate large numbers of processors and reduce significantly the execution time of many practical applications.

Chapter 7 studied the method used to choose migrants and the individuals that they replace in the receiving deme. The chapter showed that some migration policies may cause the algorithm to converge faster. The migration policy that accelerates convergence the most is to choose both the migrants and the replacements according to their fitness, which is a very common policy. The faster convergence may explain some of the controversial claims of superlinear speedups in parallel GAs. In addition, the chapter included calculations of the higher moments of the distribution of fitness. These calculations showed that the degree of the topology and the migration rate affect the population in different ways, even if they result in the same selection intensity.

Chapter 8 has a brief review of fine-grained parallel GAs. These algorithms have an interesting behavior, but have not been studied as much as the other types of parallel GAs. Fine-grained GAs can be used effectively by themselves or as a component of hierarchical algorithms. Chapter 8 described different types of hierarchical parallel GAs, and examined the question of how to choose the fastest configuration when multiple demes are combined with master-slaves. In an ideal situation, there would be enough processors available to use the optimal number of demes (r^*) and the optimal number of slaves (S). In this case, the speedup of the best hybrid parallel GA would be the product of the speedup of the optimal master-slave GA by the speedup of the optimal multi-deme. More often, there are not enough processors to implement the best configuration, and those that are available have to be distributed carefully between demes and slaves to obtain the combination that minimizes the execution time. The chapter presented a method that integrates the theory introduced earlier to find the optimal distribution of processors.

When communications are expensive relative to computations, the best algorithm will have few slaves and many demes, because the master-slave GA communicates often. As computations become more costly, the best hierarchical configurations will likely have more slaves per deme.

The last chapter also contained a complete step-by-step example that illustrated how to apply the theory presented in this book to a particular problem. The example discussed how to determine the domain-dependent constants present in the equations, and it used the method described earlier to find the best combination of demes and slaves.

2 EXTENSIONS

Although this book considered many salient issues in the design of parallel GAs, the research can be extended in several important directions. This section lists a few ideas for future research; some of them are concrete short-term projects, while others are more speculative and may guide long-term research.

There are multiple opportunities to extend the basic gambler's ruin model that we used to find appropriate population and deme sizes. For example, the model could be extended to consider crossover, mutation, and other selection methods besides tournaments. Considering the effect of selection on the population size is particularly important, because a higher selection pressure results in faster convergence, but the GA requires a larger population to succeed, so there must be an optimal setting. This tradeoff affects the multiple-deme algorithms as well, because, as we saw in the previous chapter, migration may increase the selection pressure.

The modeling of selection intensity should be extended to include the effect of the operators. The operators also affect the variance and the higher moments of the distribution of fitness. This extension is certainly a difficult task, as it must consider the fitness function, but the benefits would be great (e.g., to help balance the selection mechanism with the appropriate variation operators).

The study of multi-population algorithms can also be extended in multiple directions. For instance, the book considered algorithms that bounded the *frequency* of migration: it occurred either after convergence or every generation. However, many users of multi-deme GAs set migrations to occur every few generations, and the question of how often to migrate is still unanswered. Future research could formulate Markov chain or approximate models of frequent migration to study the effects of the frequency and rate of migration.

Another promising area could be to study topologies that adapt to the search. For example, we saw in Chapter 7 that the fitness variance decreases less dramatically when a deme has more neighbors, so the system could adapt to a rapid decrease in diversity by increasing the number of neighbors of a deme (or by modifying the migration rate). If this adaptation is done correctly, it would ease or eliminate some of the decisions about the topology that are currently in the users' hands. The models derived in this book would be a starting point to construct heuristics for this adaptation.

One of the most important areas of future research is to characterize the classes of functions where multiple populations are advantageous.

Whitley, Rana, and Heckendorn (1999) have made some progress on this question regarding separable functions, but much remains to be done.

The physical separation of populations seems a natural match to some types of problems. In particular, when we need to identify multiple solutions in multi-modal (and in multi-objective) problems, traditionally we extend a simple GA with niching techniques (Mahfoud, 1995). Some of these techniques restrict the mating or selection to subsets of similar individuals. Implementing these restrictions can be facilitated by using multiple populations and restricting migration (or the incorporation of migrants). Zavanella, Giani, and Baiardi (1998) demonstrated how to avoid wasteful computations by forcing the demes to maintain different niches. Their method could be incorporated in a future algorithm.

Fine-grained parallel GAs have not been studied much. We need a better understanding of these algorithms to use them with confidence as stand-alone problem solvers or as components of hierarchical parallel GAs. Some fundamental questions such as the size of the population and the shape of the mesh still remain unanswered. Another open area for future research is to calculate the selection intensity of different selection schemes used in fine-grained parallel EAs. This would permit to compare directly the selection pressure across different types of parallel EAs.

Having the population distributed on a mesh suggests many opportunities. For example, the neighborhoods could change shape or size dynamically, perhaps based on some measure of diversity or performance. Simple changes to the mesh have the potential of great consequences to the algorithm. For example, adding links (randomly, perhaps) between non-adjacent nodes of the graph would shorten its diameter, and would certainly impact the selection pressure (see Rudolph (2000a) for a bound of the takeover time based on the diameter). Along the same lines, deleting links between adjacent nodes would slow down the diffusion of solutions across the population, and would increase the isolation of some areas, perhaps leading to greater differentiation of solutions in the population.

Kirley and Green (2000) reported some interesting results when individuals are deleted randomly, simulating catastrophes on the geographical landscape. We could extend this idea by deleting individuals based on their fitness, for example by assigning individuals a probability of surviving the catastrophe based on their fitness. Then, a conventional selection algorithm could be used on the individuals affected by the catastrophe. We could imagine situations where the selection takes into account the entire population (think of a catastrophe hitting the entire landscape), or only a restricted section as in Kirley and Green's algorithm. Deleting individuals based on fitness may accelerate the re-colonization of the empty spaces in the landscape, which may be more efficient.

This book dealt with the parallelization of simple GAs, which have been used successfully to solve difficult problems in many areas. But simple GAs suffer from an important problem: unless related variables are encoded close to each other in the chromosome, the algorithm has an exponential time complexity (Thierens & Goldberg, 1993; Thierens, 1995). More recent GAs try to learn the structure of the problem by estimating a probabilistic model of the promising individuals (Pelikan et al., 1999; Mühlenbein & Mahnig, 1999; Etxeberria & Larrañaga, 1999). Instead of using crossover and mutation, these modern GAs use the probabilistic model to generate new individuals. Parallelizing these algorithms with a master-slave approach is trivial, and the analysis of this book would be the same. In addition, we could think of using multiple populations and migrate individuals, or we can realize that learning a probabilistic model is a form of (lossy) compression and, instead of migrating individuals, we could communicate the models and generate as many individuals as needed. In any case, most of the analysis of this book would still hold. Some interesting extensions could be to explore ways to combine the models before generating individuals.

3 CONCLUSIONS

This book introduced a principled methodology towards the rational design of fast parallel GAs. Practitioners and theoreticians alike can benefit from the research reported here. On one hand, theoreticians may adopt the decomposition of the complex design problem into semi-independent facets to obtain simple, useful, and accurate models of other aspects of serial or parallel GAs. Most of the contributions of this research were made possible by focusing on one facet and assuming that the others had appropriate settings or were bounded by the cases that we examined. This work demonstrates that exact or complete models are not necessary to grasp the effects of the problem's difficulty and the parameters of parallel GAs on quality and efficiency.

On the other hand, practitioners no longer need to use blind guessing or expensive systematic experimentation to determine the size and number of demes or how to connect them. Instead, they can use the tools developed here to choose a configuration that yields good results fast and reliably. Some experimentation is necessary to calibrate the models to the particular domain and hardware environment, but these experiments are cheap and easy to perform.

We must be cautious, however, and recognize that the models presented here have limitations. Most importantly, we only considered additively-decomposable functions, and most of the models are based on the solution to the gambler's ruin, which makes some simplifying assumptions that are listed in Chapter 2. Other assumptions that are particular to specific models are listed in the chapters that introduced the models.

In concrete, this book made the following contributions to our understanding of parallel GAs:

Accurate population sizing for simple and parallel GAs. A GA needs an adequate population size to be both effective and efficient. The gambler's ruin model for simple GAs (introduced by Harik et al. (1997)) and its extensions to parallel GAs enable the adequately sizing of populations to reach solutions of arbitrary quality on particular domains.

Similar scalability of single and multiple demes. Master-slaves and several bounding cases of multiple communicating demes have asymptotically the same optimal processor count: $\mathcal{P}^* = O(\sqrt{\frac{nT_f}{T_c}})$. This means that regardless of their type (single or multiple populations), parallel GAs can integrate large numbers of processors. Although for a long time parallel GAs have been regarded as highly scalable, the closed-form expressions of $\mathcal{P}^*$ permit to quantify those claims taking into account the specific problem domain and the hardware platform.

Lower bound on acceptable parallelism. With very simple calculations users can determine the minimum benefits they can expect from parallel implementations. An objective evaluation of the potential benefits can be very useful to make the decision of implementing a parallel GA.

Isolated demes seem impractical. Users should avoid this extreme case of parallel GAs, because the savings on execution time seem only marginal.

Migration greatly improves quality and efficiency. The solution quality improves greatly after the second epoch, and in the limit it approaches the quality that an aggregate panmictic population would reach. With higher average qualities per deme, their sizes can be reduced to obtain significant savings on the execution time.

Fully-connected topologies may be adequate. Although it is not scalable, this topology reduces the execution time significantly using few demes. Fully-connected topologies may be the best choice when a small number of processors are available.

Varying migration rates. In general, higher migration rates result in better solutions, but even moderately low rates are sufficient to reach solutions of the same quality as a panmictic population.

Effect of topologies. Dense topologies result in better solutions because there are more potential sources of BBs, but they are also more costly than sparse topologies. This book showed how to quantify the increases in quality and cost, and how to choose a topology that minimizes the effort while still reaching the desired solution.

Migration may cause faster convergence. Selecting migrants and replacements according to their fitness (as opposed to choosing them randomly) increases the speed of convergence. Although this is desirable, we must be aware that the algorithm may converge too fast to a suboptimal solution. One possible solution suggested by another result of this book is to increase the population size according to the selection pressure.

Explanation of superlinear speedups. The acceleration of convergence caused by migration is a possible explanation of the controversial claims of superlinear speedups.

Optimal allocation of available resources. The models introduced in this book can be used to determine the number of demes, their size, their connectivity, and the number of slaves per deme that reach the desired solution with the minimum cost.

While there is much work needed to fully comprehend all facets of parallel GAs, the results from this research constitute a collection of ideas that expand our knowledge of these algorithms. They should be incorporated into projects that use parallel GAs to improve both solution quality and algorithmic efficiency.

References

Abramowitz, M., & Stegun, I. (1972). *Handbook of mathematical functions with formulas, graphs, and mathematical tables.* New York: Dover Publications.

Abramson, D., & Abela, J. (1992). A parallel genetic algorithm for solving the school timetabling problem. In *Proceedings of the Fifteenth Australian Computer Science Conference (ACSC-15),* Volume 14 (pp. 1–11).

Abramson, D., Mills, G., & Perkins, S. (1993). Parallelisation of a genetic algorithm for the computation of efficient train schedules. In *Proceedings of the 1993 Parallel Computing and Transputers Conference* (pp. 139–149).

Adamidis, P. (1994). *Review of parallel genetic algorithms bibliography* (Tech. Rep. Version 1). Thessaloniki, Greece: Aristotle University of Thessaloniki.

Adamidis, P., & Petridis, V. (1996). Co-operating populations with different evolution behaviours. In Bäck, T., Kitano, H., & Michalewicz, Z. (Eds.), *Proceedings of the 1996 IEEE International Conference on Evolutionary Computation* (pp. 188–191). Piscataway, NJ: IEEE Service Center.

Alba, E., & Troya, J. M. (1999). A survey of parallel distributed genetic algorithms. *Complexity, 4*(4), 31–52.

Almasi, G. S., & Gottlieb, A. (1994). *Highly parallel computing* (2nd ed.). Benjamin/Cummings Publishing Company.

Anderson, E. J., & Ferris, M. C. (1990). A genetic algorithm for the assembly line balancing problem. In *Integer Programming and Combinatorial Optimization: Proceedings of a 1990 Conference Held at the University of Waterloo* (pp. 7–18). Waterloo, ON: University of Waterloo Press.

Andre, D., & Koza, J. R. (1998). A parallel implementation of genetic programming that achieves super-linear performance. *Journal of Information Sciences, 106,* 201–218.

Bäck, T. (1994a). Parallel optimization of evolutionary algorithms. In Davidor, Y., Schwefel, H.-P., & Männer, R. (Eds.), *Parallel Problem Solving fron Nature, PPSN III* (pp. 418–427). Berlin: Springer-Verlag.

Bäck, T. (1994b). Selective pressure in evolutionary algorithms: A characterization of selection mechanisms. In *Proceedings of the First IEEE Conference on Evolutionary Computation,* Volume 1 (pp. 57–62). Piscataway, NJ: IEEE Service Center.

Bäck, T. (1995). Generalized convergence models for tournament- and (μ, λ)-selection. In Eschelman, L. (Ed.), *Proceedings of the Sixth International Conference on Genetic Algorithms* (pp. 2–8). San Francisco, CA: Morgan Kaufmann.

Bäck, T. (1996). *Evolutionary algorithms in theory and practice.* New York: Oxford University Press.

Baker, J. E. (1985). Adaptive selection methods for genetic algorithms. In Grefenstette, J. J. (Ed.), *Proceedings of an International Conference on Genetic Algorithms and Their Applications* (pp. 101–111). Hillsdale, NJ: Lawrence Erlbaum Associates.

Baker, J. E. (1987). Reducing bias and ineffiency in the selection algorithm. In Grefenstette, J. J. (Ed.), *Proceedings of the Second International Conference on Genetic Algorithms* (pp. 14–21). Hillsdale, NJ: Lawrence Erlbaum Associates.

Baluja, S. (1992). *A massively distributed parallel genetic algorithm (mdpGA)* (Tech. Rep. No. CMU-CS-92-196R). Pittsburgh, PA: Carnegie Mellon University.

Baluja, S. (1993). Structure and performance of fine-grain parallelism in genetic search. In Forrest, S. (Ed.), *Proceedings of the Fifth International Conference on Genetic Algorithms* (pp. 155–162). San Mateo, CA: Morgan Kaufmann.

Baluja, S. (1994). *Population-based incremental learning: A method for integrating genetic search based function optimization and competitive learning* (Tech. Rep. No. CMU-CS-94-163). Pittsburgh, PA: Carnegie Mellon University.

Belding, T. C. (1995). The distributed genetic algorithm revisited. In Eschelman, L. (Ed.), *Proceedings of the Sixth International Conference on Genetic Algorithms* (pp. 114–121). San Francisco, CA: Morgan Kaufmann.

Bennett III, F. H., Koza, J. R., Shipman, J., & Stiffelman, O. (1999). Building a parallel computer system for $18,000 that performs a half peta-flob per day. In Banzhaf, W., Daida, J., Eiben, A. E., Garzon, M. H., Honavar, V., Jakiela, M., & Smith, R. E. (Eds.), *GECCO-99: Proceedings of the Genetic and Evolutionary Computation Conference* (pp. 1484–1490). San Francisco, CA: Morgan Kaufmann.

Bethke, A. D. (1976). *Comparison of genetic algorithms and gradient-based optimizers on parallel processors: Efficiency of use of processing capacity* (Tech. Rep. No. 197). Ann Arbor, MI: University of Michigan, Logic of Computers Group.

Beyer, H.-G. (1993). Toward a theory of evolution strategies: Some asymptotical results from the $(1\dagger\lambda)$-Theory. *Evolutionary computation, 1*(2), 165–188.

Bianchini, R., & Brown, C. M. (1993). Parallel genetic algorithms on distributed-memory architectures. In Atkins, S., & Wagner, A. S. (Eds.), *Transputer Research and Applications 6* (pp. 67–82). Amsterdam: IOS Press.

Blickle, T., & Thiele, L. (1996). A comparison of selection schemes used in evolutionary algorithms. *Evolutionary Computation, 4*(4), 361–394.

Booker, L. B. (1982). *Intelligent behavior as an adaptation to the task environment.* Unpublished doctoral dissertation, The University of Michigan. (University Microfilms No. 8214966).

Bossert, W. (1967). Mathematical optimization: Are there abstract limits on natural selection? In Moorehead, P. S., & Kaplan, M. M. (Eds.), *Mathematical Challenges to the Neo-Darwinian Interpretation of Evolution* (pp. 35–46). Philadelphia, PA: The Wistar Institute Press.

Branke, J., Andersen, H. C., & Schmeck, H. (1996). Global selection methods for massively parallel computers. In Fogarty, T. C. (Ed.), *Proceedings of the AISB'96 Workshop on Evolutionary Computing* (pp. 175–188). Berlin: Springer-Verlag. Lecture Notes in Computer Science 1143.

Braud, A., & Vrain, C. (1999, July). A parallel genetic algorithm based on the BSP model. In *Evolutionary Computation and Parallel Processing Workshop, Proceedings of the 1999 GECCO Workshops.*

Braun, H. C. (1990). On solving travelling salesman problems by genetic algorithms. In Schwefel, H.-P., & Männer, R. (Eds.), *Parallel Problem Solving from Nature* (pp. 129–133). Berlin: Springer-Verlag.

Brindle, A. (1981). *Genetic algorithms for function optimization.* Unpublished doctoral dissertation, University of Alberta, Edmonton, Canada.

Burrows, P. (1972). Expected selection differentials for directional selection. *Biometrics, 23,* 1091–1100.

Calégari, P. R. (1999). *Parallelization of population-based evolutionary algorithms for combinatorial optimization problems.* Unpublished doctoral dissertation, École Polytechnique Fédérale de Lausanne (EPFL).

Cantú-Paz, E. (1998a). A survey of parallel genetic algorithms. *Calculateurs Parallèles, Reseaux et Systems Repartis, 10*(2), 141–171.

Cantú-Paz, E. (1998b). Using Markov chains to analyze a bounding case of parallel genetic algorithms. In Koza, J. R., Banzhaf, W., Chellapilla, K., Deb, K. Dorigo, M., Fogel, D. B., Garzon, M. H., Goldberg, D. E., Iba, H., & Riolo, R. L. (Eds.), *Genetic Programming 1998: Proceedings of the Third Annual Conference* (pp. 456–462). San Francisco, CA: Morgan Kaufmann.

Cantú-Paz, E. (1999a). *Designing efficient and accurate parallel genetic algorithms*. Unpublished doctoral dissertation, University of Illinois at Urbana-Champaign. Also available as IlliGAL Technical Report No. 99017.

Cantú-Paz, E. (1999b). Migration policies and takeover times in parallel genetic algorithms. In Banzhaf, W., Daida, J., Eiben, A. E., Garzon, M. H., Honavar, V., Jakiela, M., & Smith, R. E. (Eds.), *GECCO-99: Proceedings of the Genetic and Evolutionary Computation Conference* (pp. 775). San Francisco, CA: Morgan Kaufmann.

Cantú-Paz, E. (1999c). Topologies, migration rates, and multi-population parallel genetic algorithms. In Banzhaf, W., Daida, J., Eiben, A. E., Garzon, M. H., Honavar, V., Jakiela, M., & Smith, R. E. (Eds.), *GECCO-99: Proceedings of the Genetic and Evolutionary Computation Conference* (pp. 91–98). San Francisco, CA: Morgan Kaufmann.

Cantú-Paz, E. (2000a). Markov chain models of parallel genetic algorithms. *IEEE Transactions on Evolutionary Computation, 4*(3). Also available as IlliGAL Report No. 98010.

Cantú-Paz, E. (2000b). On the effects of migration on the fitness distribution of parallel evolutionary algorithms. In Wu, A. (Ed.), *Evolutionary Computation and Parallel Processing Workshop, Proceedings of the GECCO-2000 Workshops* (pp. 3–6).

Cantú-Paz, E. (2000c). Selection intensity in genetic algorithms with generation gaps. In Whitley, D., Goldberg, D. E., Cantú-Paz, E., Spector, L., Parmee, I., & Beyer, H.-G. (Eds.), *GECCO-2000: Proceedings of the Genetic and Evolutionary Computation Conference* (pp. 911–918). San Francisco, CA: Morgan Kaufmann.

Cantú-Paz, E. (In Press). Migration policies, selection pressure, and parallel evolutionary algorithms. *Journal of Heuristics*. Also available as IlliGAL Report No. 99015.

Cantú-Paz, E., & Goldberg, D. E. (1997a). Modeling idealized bounding cases of parallel genetic algorithms. In Koza, J., Deb, K., Dorigo, M., Fogel, D., Garzon, M., Iba, H., & Riolo, R. (Eds.), *Genetic Programming 1997: Proceedings of the Second Annual Conference* (pp. 353–361). San Francisco, CA: Morgan Kaufmann.

Cantú-Paz, E., & Goldberg, D. E. (1997b). Predicting speedups of idealized bounding cases of parallel genetic algorithms. In Bäck, T. (Ed.), *Proceedings of the Seventh International Conference on Genetic Algorithms* (pp. 113–120). San Francisco: Morgan Kaufmann.

Cantú-Paz, E., & Goldberg, D. E. (1999). On the scalability of parallel genetic algorithms. *Evolutionary Computation, 7*(4), 429–449.

Cantú-Paz, E., & Goldberg, D. E. (2000). Efficient parallel genetic algorithms: theory and practice. *Computer Methods in Applied Mechanics and Engineering, 186*, 221–238.

Cantú-Paz, E., & Mejía-Olvera, M. (1994). Experimental results in distributed genetic algorithms. In *International Symposium on Applied Corporate Computing* (pp. 99–108). Monterrey, Mexico.

Capcarrère, M., Tomassini, M., Tettamanzi, A., & Sipper, M. (1999). A statistical study of a class of cellular evolutionary algorithms. *Evolutionary Computation*, *7*(3), 255–274.

Chakraborty, U. K., Deb, K., & Chakraborty, M. (1996). Analysis of selection algorithms: A Markov chain approach. *Evolutionary Computation*, *4*(2), 133–167.

Chong, F.-S. (1999, July). Java-based distributed genetic programming on the internet. In Wu, A. (Ed.), *Evolutionary Computation and Parallel Processing Workshop, Proceedings of the 1999 GECCO Workshops* (pp. 163–166).

Cohoon, J. P., Hegde, S. U., Martin, W. N., & Richards, D. (1987). Punctuated equilibria: A parallel genetic algorithm. In Grefenstette, J. J. (Ed.), *Proceedings of the Second International Conference on Genetic Algorithms* (pp. 148–154). Hillsdale, NJ: Lawrence Erlbaum Associates.

Cohoon, J. P., Martin, W. N., & Richards, D. S. (1991). Genetic algorithms and punctuated equilibria in VLSI. In Schwefel, H.-P., & Männer, R. (Eds.), *Parallel Problem Solving from Nature* (pp. 134–144). Berlin: Springer-Verlag.

Collins, R. J., & Jefferson, D. R. (1991). Selection in massively parallel genetic algorithms. In Belew, R. K., & Booker, L. B. (Eds.), *Proceedings of the Fourth International Conference on Genetic Algorithms* (pp. 249–256). San Mateo, CA: Morgan Kaufmann.

Cvetković, D., & Mühlenbein, H. (1994). *The optimal population size for uniform crossover and truncation selection* (Tech. Rep. No. GMD AS GA 94-11). Germany: German National Reseach Center for Computer Science (GMD).

Davidor, Y. (1993). The ECOlogical framework II: Improving GA performance at virtually zero cost. In Forrest, S. (Ed.), *Proceedings of the Fifth International Conference on Genetic Algorithms* (pp. 171–176). San Mateo, CA: Morgan Kaufmann.

Davison, B. D., & Rasheed, K. (1999, July). Effect of global parallelism on a steady state ga. In Wu, A. (Ed.), *Evolutionary Computation and Parallel Processing Workshop, Proceedings of the 1999 GECCO Workshops* (pp. 167–170).

De Jong, K. A. (1975). *An analysis of the behavior of a class of genetic adaptive systems*. Doctoral dissertation, University of Michigan, Ann Arbor. (University Microfilms No. 76-9381).

Deb, K., & Goldberg, D. E. (1993). Analyzing deception in trap functions. In Whitley, L. D. (Ed.), *Foundations of Genetic Algorithms 2* (pp. 93–108). San Mateo, CA: Morgan Kaufmann.

Deb, K., & Goldberg, D. E. (1994). Sufficient conditions for deceptive and easy binary functions. *Annals of Mathematics and Artificial Intelligence*, *10*, 385–408.

Dymek, A. (1992). *An examination of hypercube implementations of genetic algorithms*. umt, Air Force Institute of Technology, Wright-Patterson Air Force Base, OH.

Eiben, A. E., & Bäck, T. (1997). Empirical investigation of multiparent recombination operators in evolution strategies. *Evolutionary Computation*, *5*(3), 347–365.

Eiben, A. E., Raué, P.-E., & Ruttkay, Z. (1994). Genetic algorithms with multi-parent recombination. In Davidor, Y., Schwefel, H.-P., & Männer, R. (Eds.), *Parallel Problem Solving fron Nature, PPSN III* (pp. 78–87). Berlin: Springer-Verlag.

Elredge, N., & Gould, S. (1972). Punctuated equilibria: An alternative to phyletic gradualism. In Schopf, T. J. M. (Ed.), *Models in Paleobiology* (pp. 82–115). San Francisco, CA: Freeman, Cooper, and Co.

Etxeberria, R., & Larrañaga, P. (1999). Global optimization with bayesian networks. In *II Symposium on Artificial Intelligence CIMAF99. Special session on Distributions and Evolutionary Optimization* (pp. 332–339).

Feller, W. (1966). *An introduction to probability theory and its applications* (2nd ed.), Volume 1. John Wiley and Sons.

Fogarty, T. C., & Huang, R. (1991). Implementing the genetic algorithm on transputer based parallel processing systems. In Schwefel, H.-P., & Männer, R. (Eds.), *Parallel Problem Solving from Nature* (pp. 145–149). Berlin: Springer-Verlag.

Goldberg, D. E. (1987). Simple genetic algorithms and the minimal, deceptive problem. In Davis, L. (Ed.), *Genetic Algorithms and Simulated Annealing* (Chapter 6, pp. 74–88). Los Altos, CA: Morgan Kaufmann.

Goldberg, D. E. (1989a). *Genetic algorithms in search, optimization, and machine learning.* Reading, MA: Addison-Wesley.

Goldberg, D. E. (1989b). Sizing populations for serial and parallel genetic algorithms. In Schaffer, J. D. (Ed.), *Proceedings of the Third International Conference on Genetic Algorithms* (pp. 70–79). San Mateo, CA: Morgan Kaufmann. (Also TCGA Report 88004).

Goldberg, D. E. (1991). *A tutorial on genetic algorithm theory.* A presentation given at the Fourth International Conference on Genetic Algorithms, University of California at San Diego, La Jolla, CA.

Goldberg, D. E. (1992). Construction of high-order deceptive functions using low-order Walsh coefficients. *Annals of Mathematics and Artificial Intelligence, 5,* 35–48.

Goldberg, D. E. (1994). Genetic and evolutionary algorithms come of age. *Communications of the ACM, 37*(3), 113–119.

Goldberg, D. E. (1996a, June). Personal communication.

Goldberg, D. E. (1996b). The design of innovating machines: Lessons from genetic algorithms. In Désidéri, J.-A., Hirsch, C., Le Tallec, P., Oñate, E., Pandolfi, M., Périaux, J., & Stein, E. (Eds.), *Computational Methods in Applied Sciences '96* (pp. 100–104). Chichester: John Wiley & Sons.

Goldberg, D. E. (1998). Personal communication.

Goldberg, D. E., & Deb, K. (1991). A comparative analysis of selection schemes used in genetic algorithms. *Foundations of Genetic Algorithms, 1,* 69–93. (Also TCGA Report 90007).

Goldberg, D. E., Deb, K., & Clark, J. H. (1992). Genetic algorithms, noise, and the sizing of populations. *Complex Systems, 6,* 333–362.

Goldberg, D. E., Deb, K., Kargupta, H., & Harik, G. (1993). Rapid, accurate optimization of difficult problems using fast messy genetic algorithms. In Forrest, S. (Ed.), *Proceedings of the Fifth International Conference on Genetic Algorithms* (pp. 56–64). San Mateo, CA: Morgan Kaufmann.

Goldberg, D. E., Deb, K., & Thierens, D. (1993). Toward a better understanding of mixing in genetic algorithms. *Journal of the Society of Instrument and Control Engineers, 32*(1), 10–16.

Goldberg, D. E., Korb, B., & Deb, K. (1989). Messy genetic algorithms: Motivation, analysis, and first results. *Complex Systems, 3*(5), 493–530. (Also TCGA Report 89003).

Goldberg, D. E., & Rudnick, M. (1991). Genetic algorithms and the variance of fitness. *Complex Systems, 5*(3), 265–278. (Also IlliGAL Report No. 91001).

Goodman, E. D., Averill, R. C., Punch, W. F., & Eby, D. J. (1997). *Parallel genetic algorithms in the optimization of composite structures* (GARAGe 97-05-02). East Lansing, MI: Genetic Algorithms Research and Applications Group, Michigan State University.

Gordon, V. S. (1994). Locality in genetic algorithms. In *Proceedings of the First IEEE Conference on Evolutionary Computation*, Volume 1 (pp. 428–432). Piscataway, NJ: IEEE Service Center.

Gordon, V. S., & Whitley, D. (1993). Serial and parallel genetic algorithms as function optimizers. In Forrest, S. (Ed.), *Proceedings of the Fifth International Conference on Genetic Algorithms* (pp. 177–183). San Mateo, CA: Morgan Kaufmann.

Gordon, V. S., Whitley, D., & Böhm, A. P. W. (1992). Dataflow parallelism in genetic algorithms. In Männer, R., & Manderick, B. (Eds.), *Parallel Problem Solving from Nature, 2* (pp. 533–542). Amsterdam: Elsevier Science.

Gorges-Schleuter, M. (1989). ASPARAGOS: A population genetics approach to genetic algorithms. In Voigt, H.-M., Mühlenbein, H., & Schwefel, H.-P. (Eds.), *Evolution and Optimization '89* (pp. 86–94). Berlin: Akademie-Verlag.

Gorges-Schleuter, M. (1989). ASPARAGOS: An asynchronous parallel genetic optimization strategy. In Schaffer, J. D. (Ed.), *Proceedings of the Third International Conference on Genetic Algorithms* (pp. 422–428). San Mateo, CA: Morgan Kaufmann.

Gorges-Schleuter, M. (1991). Explicit parallelism of genetic algorithms through population structures. In Schwefel, H.-P., & Männer, R. (Eds.), *Parallel Problem Solving from Nature* (pp. 150–159). Berlin: Springer-Verlag.

Gorges-Schleuter, M. (1992). Comparison of local mating strategies in massively parallel genetic algorithms. In Männer, R., & Manderick, B. (Eds.), *Parallel Problem Solving from Nature, 2* (pp. 553–562). Amsterdam: Elsevier Science.

Gorges-Schleuter, M. (1997). Asparagos96 and the traveling salesman problem. In Bäck, T. (Ed.), *Proceedings of the Fourth International Conference on Evolutionary Computation* (pp. 171–174). New York: IEEE Press.

Gorges-Schleuter, M. (1998). A comparitive study of global and local selection in evolution strategies. In Eiben, A. E., Bäck, T., Schoenauer, M., & Schwefel, H.-P. (Eds.), *Parallel Problem Solving from Nature, PPSN V* (pp. 367–377). Berlin: Springer-Verlag.

Gorges-Schleuter, M. (1999). An analysis of local selection in evolution strategies. In Banzhaf, W., Daida, J., Eiben, A. E., Garzon, M. H., Honavar, V., Jakiela, M., & Smith, R. E. (Eds.), *Proceedings of the Genetic and Evolutionary Computati on Conference* (pp. 847–854). San Francisco, CA: Morgan Kaufmann.

Grefenstette, J. J. (1981). *Parallel adaptive algorithms for function optimization* (Tech. Rep. No. CS-81-19). Nashville, TN: Vanderbilt University, Computer Science Department.

Grefenstette, J. J. (1992). Genetic algorithms for changing environments. In Männer, R., & Manderick, B. (Eds.), *Parallel Problem Solving from Nature, 2* (pp. 137–144). Amsterdam: Elsevier Science.

Grefenstette, J. J. (1995). Robot learning with parallel genetic algorithms on networked computers. In Oren, T., & Birta, L. (Eds.), *Proceedings of the 1995 Summer Computer Simulation Conference (SCSC 95)* (pp. 352–357). Ottawa: The Society for Computer Simulation.

Grosso, P. B. (1985). *Computer simulations of genetic adaptation: Parallel subcomponent interaction in a multilocus model.* Unpublished doctoral dissertation, The University of Michigan. (University Microfilms No. 8520908).

Gruau, F. (1994). *Neural network synthesis using cellular encoding and the genetic algorithm.* Unpublished doctoral dissertation, L'Universite Claude Bernard-Lyon I.

Gwo, J.-P., Hoffman, F., & Hargrove, W. (2000). Mechanistic-based genetic algorithm search on a Beowulf cluster of Linux PCs. In *Proceedings of the High Performance Computing Conference*. Washington, DC.

Hancock, P. J. B. (1997). Selection: a comparison of selection mechanisms. In Bäck, T., Fogel, D. B., & Michalewicz, Z. (Eds.), *Handbook of Evolutionary Computation* (pp. C2.8:1–C2.8:11). Bristol and New York: Institute of Physics Publishing and Oxford University Press.

Harik, G. (1999). *Linkage learning via probabilistic modeling in the ECGA* (IlliGAL Report No. 99010). Urbana, IL: University of Illinois at Urbana-Champaign, Illinois Genetic Algorithms Laboratory.

Harik, G., Cantú-Paz, E., Goldberg, D., & Miller, B. L. (1997). The gambler's ruin problem, genetic algorithms, and the sizing of populations. In Bäck, T. (Ed.), *Proceedings of the Fourth International Conference on Evolutionary Computation* (pp. 7–12). New York: IEEE Press.

Harik, G., Cantú-Paz, E., Goldberg, D., & Miller, B. L. (1999). The gambler's ruin problem, genetic algorithms, and the sizing of populations. *Evolutionary Computation*, *7*(3), 231–253.

Harik, G. R., & Goldberg, D. E. (1996). Learning linkage. In Belew, R. K., & Vose, M. D. (Eds.), *Foundations of Genetic Algorithms 4* (pp. 247–262). San Francisco: Morgan Kaufmann.

Harik, G. R., Lobo, F. G., & Goldberg, D. E. (1998). The compact genetic algorithm. In *Proceedings of the 1998 IEEE International Conference on Evolutionary Computation* (pp. 523–528). Piscataway, NJ: IEEE Service Center.

Hart, W. E. (1994). *Adaptive global optimization with local search*. Doctoral dissertation, University of California, San Diego.

Hart, W. E., Baden, S., Belew, R. K., & Kohn, S. (1996). Analysis of the numerical effects of parallelism on a parallel genetic algorithm. In *Proceedings of the 10th International Parallel Processing Symposium* (pp. 606–612). IEEE Press.

Harter, H. L. (1970). *Order statistics and their use in testing and estimation*. Washington, D.C.: U.S. Government Printing Office.

Hauser, R., & Männer, R. (1994). Implementation of standard genetic algorithm on MIMD machines. In Davidor, Y., Schwefel, H.-P., & Männer, R. (Eds.), *Parallel Problem Solving fron Nature, PPSN III* (pp. 504–513). Berlin: Springer-Verlag.

Herrera, F., & Lozano, M. (2000). Gradual distributed real-coded genetic algorithms. *IEEE Transactions on Evolutionary Computation*, *4*(1), 43–63.

Hillis, D. (1985). *The connection machine*. Cambridge, MA: MIT Press.

Hirsh, J., & Young, D. (1998). Evolutionary programming strategies with self adaptation applied to the design of rotorcraft using parallel processing. In Porto, V. W., Saravanan, N., Waagen, D., & Eiben, A. (Eds.), *Proceedings of the Seventh Annual Conference on Evolutionary Programming* (pp. 147–156). Berlin: Springer Verlag.

Holland, J. H. (1973). Genetic algorithms and the optimal allocation of trials. *SIAM Journal on Computing*, *2*(2), 88–105.

Holland, J. H. (1975). *Adaptation in natural and artificial systems*. Ann Arbor, MI: University of Michigan Press.

Isaacson, D. L., & Madsen, R. W. (1976). *Markov chains theory and applications*. New York, NY: John Wiley and Sons, Inc.

Kargupta, H. (1996). The gene expression messy genetic algorithm. In Bäck, T., Kitano, H., & Michalewicz, Z. (Eds.), *Proceedings of the 1996 IEEE International Conference on Evolutionary Computation* (pp. 814–819). Piscataway, NJ: IEEE Service Center.

Kirley, M. (2000). An empirical investigation of optimisation in dynamic environments using the cellular genetic algorithm. In Whitley, D., Goldberg, D. E., Cantú-Paz, E., Spector, L., Parmee, I., & Beyer, H.-G. (Eds.), *GECCO-2000: Proceedings of the Genetic and Evolutionary Computation Conference* (pp. 11–18). San Francisco, CA: Morgan Kaufmann.

Kirley, M., & Green, D. G. (2000). Adaptation and spatial patterns: Optimization using the cellular genetic algorithm. In Wu, A. S. (Ed.), *Proceedings of the 2000 Genetic and Evolutionary Computation Conference Workshop Program* (pp. 12–16).

Koza, J. R., & Andre, D. (1995). *Parallel genetic programming on a network of transputers* (Tech. Rep. No. STAN-CS-TR-95-1542). Stanford, CA: Stanford University.

Koza, J. R., David Andre, Bennett III, F. H., & Keane, M. (1999). *Genetic programming III: Darwinian invention and problem solving.* San Francisco, CA: Morgan Kaufmann.

Kröger, B., Schwenderling, P., & Vornberger, O. (1991). Parallel genetic packing of rectangles. In Schwefel, H.-P., & Männer, R. (Eds.), *Parallel Problem Solving from Nature* (pp. 160–164). Berlin: Springer-Verlag.

Kröger, B., Schwenderling, P., & Vornberger, O. (1992). Massive parallel genetic packing. *Transputing in Numerical and Neural Network Applications*, 214–230.

Kröger, B., Schwenderling, P., & Vornberger, O. (1993). Parallel genetic packing on transputers. In Stender, J. (Ed.), *Parallel Genetic Algorithms: Theory and Applications* (pp. 151–185). Amsterdam: IOS Press.

Levine, D. (1994). *A parallel genetic algorithm for the set partitioning problem.* Doctoral dissertation, Illinois Institute of Technology. Also available as Technical Report Argonne Natl Lab ANL-94/23.

Lin, S.-C., Goodman, E. D., & Punch III, W. F. (1997). Investigating parallel genetic algorithms on job shop scheduling problems. In Angeline, P. J., Reynolds, R. G., McDonnell, J. R., & Eberhart, R. (Eds.), *Evolutionary Programming VI* (pp. 383–393). Berlin: Springer.

Lin, S.-C., Punch, W., & Goodman, E. (1994, October). Coarse-grain parallel genetic algorithms: Categorization and new approach. In *Sixth IEEE Symposium on Parallel and Distributed Processing.* Los Alamitos, CA: IEEE Computer Society Press.

Mahfoud, S. W. (1995, May). *Niching methods for genetic algorithms.* Unpublished doctoral dissertation, University of Illinois at Urbana-Champaign, Urbana, IL. Also IlliGAL Report No. 95001.

Manderick, B., & Spiessens, P. (1989). Fine-grained parallel genetic algorithms. In Schaffer, J. D. (Ed.), *Proceedings of the Third International Conference on Genetic Algorithms* (pp. 428–433). San Mateo, CA: Morgan Kaufmann.

Merkle, L. D., Gates, G. H., & Lamont, G. B. (1998). Scalability of an MPI-based fast messy genetic algorithm. In et al., C. (Ed.), *Proceedings of the 1998 Symposium on Applied Computing* (pp. 386–393). New York, NY: Association for Computing Machinery.

Merkle, L. D., & Lamont, G. B. (1993). Comparison of parallel messy genetic algorithm data distribution strategies. In Forrest, S. (Ed.), *Proceedings of the Fifth International Conference on Genetic Algorithms* (pp. 191–198). San Mateo, CA: Morgan Kaufmann.

Miller, B. L. (1997). *Noise, sampling, and efficient genetic algorithms.* Doctoral dissertation, University of Illinois at Urbana-Champaign. Also available as IlliGAL tech report No. 97001.

Miller, B. L., & Goldberg, D. E. (1995). Genetic algorithms, tournament selection, and the effects of noise. *Complex Systems*, *9*(3), 193–212.

Miller, B. L., & Goldberg, D. E. (1996). Genetic algorithms, selection schemes, and the varying effects of noise. *Evolutionary Computation*, *4*(2), 113–131.

Mühlenbein, H. (1989a). Parallel genetic algorithms, population genetics, and combinatorial optimization. In Voigt, H.-M., Mühlenbein, H., & Schwefel, H.-P. (Eds.), *Evolution and Optimization '89* (pp. 79–85). Berlin: Akademie-Verlag.

Mühlenbein, H. (1989b). Parallel genetic algorithms, population genetics and combinatorial optimization. In Schaffer, J. D. (Ed.), *Proceedings of the Third International Conference on Genetic Algorithms* (pp. 416–421). San Mateo, CA: Morgan Kaufmann.

Mühlenbein, H. (1991). Evolution in time and space-The parallel genetic algorithm. In Rawlins, G. J. E. (Ed.), *Foundations of Genetic Algorithms* (pp. 316–337). San Mateo, CA: Morgan Kaufmann.

Mühlenbein, H., & Mahnig, T. (1999). FDA–a scalable evolutionary algorithm for the optimization of additively decomposable functions. *Evolutionary Computation*, *7*(4), 353–376.

Mühlenbein, H., & Paaß, G. (1996). From recombination of genes to the estimation of distributions I. Binary parameters. In Voigt, H.-M., Ebeling, W., Rechenberg, I., & Schwefel, H.-P. (Eds.), *Parallel Problem Solving from Nature, PPSN IV* (pp. 178–187). Berlin: Springer-Verlag.

Mühlenbein, H., & Schlierkamp-Voosen, D. (1993). Predictive models for the breeder genetic algorithm: I. Continuous parameter optimization. *Evolutionary Computation*, *1*(1), 25–49.

Mühlenbein, H., & Schlierkamp-Voosen, D. (1994). The science of breeding and its application to the breeder genetic algorithm (BGA). *Evolutionary Computation*, *1*(4), 335–360.

Mühlenbein, H., Schomisch, M., & Born, J. (1991). The parallel genetic algorithm as function optimizer. In Belew, R. K., & Booker, L. B. (Eds.), *Proceedings of the Fourth International Conference on Genetic Algorithms* (pp. 271–278). San Mateo, CA: Morgan Kaufmann.

Munetomo, M., Takai, Y., & Sato, Y. (1993). An efficient migration scheme for subpopulation-based asynchronously parallel genetic algorithms. In Forrest, S. (Ed.), *Proceedings of the Fifth International Conference on Genetic Algorithms* (pp. 649). San Mateo, CA: Morgan Kaufmann.

Nangsue, P., & Conry, S. E. (1998). An agent-oriented, massively distributed parallelization model of evolutionary algorithms. In Koza, J. R. (Ed.), *Late Breaking Papers at the Genetic Programming 1998 Conference* (pp. 160–168). Madison, WI.

Norman, M. (1989). *A genetic approach to topology optimisation for multiprocessor architectures*. Unpublished manuscript.

Nowostawski, M., & Poli, R. (1999). Dynamic demes parallel genetic algorithm. In *Proceedings of Third International Conference on Knowledge-based Intelligent Information Engineering Systems, KES'99*. Preliminary version avalable as Technical Report CSRP-99-12, School of Computer Science, University of Birmingham.

Ochoa, G., Harvey, I., & Buxton, H. (2000). Optimal mutation rates and selection pressure in genetic algorithms. In Whitley, D., Goldberg, D. E., Cantú-Paz, E., Spector, L., Parmee, I., & Beyer, H.-G. (Eds.), *GECCO-2000: Proceedings of the Genetic and Evolutionary Computation Conference* (pp. 315–322). San Francisco, CA: Morgan Kaufmann.

Oppacher, F., & Wineberg, M. (1999). The shifting balance genetic algorithm: Improving the GA in a dynamic environment. In Banzhaf, W., Daida, J., Eiben, A. E., Garzon, M. H., Honavar, V., Jakiela, M., & Smith, R. E. (Eds.), *Proceedings of the Genetic and Evolutionary Computation Conference* (pp. 504–510). San Francisco, CA: Morgan Kaufmann.

Oussaidène, M. (1997). *Genetic programming methodology, parallelization and applications.* Unpublished doctoral dissertation, Université de Genève, Genève.

Pelikan, M., Goldberg, D. E., & Cantú-Paz, E. (1999). BOA: The Bayesian optimization algorithm. In Banzhaf, W., Daida, J., Eiben, A. E., Garzon, M. H., Honavar, V., Jakiela, M., & Smith, R. E. (Eds.), *GECCO-99: Proceedings of the 1999 Genetic and Evolutionary Computation Conference* (pp. 525–532). San Francisco, CA: Morgan Kaufmann.

Pettey, C. B., Leuze, M. R., & Grefenstette, J. J. (1987). A parallel genetic algorithm. In Grefenstette, J. J. (Ed.), *Proceedings of the Second International Conference on Genetic Algorithms* (pp. 155–161). Hillsdale, NJ: Lawrence Erlbaum Associates.

Pettey, C. C. (1997). Population structures: diffusion (cellular) models. In Bäck, T., Fogel, D. B., & Michalewicz, Z. (Eds.), *Handbook of Evolutionary Computation* (pp. C6.4:1–C6.4:6). Bristol and New York: Institute of Physics Publishing and Oxford University Press.

Pettey, C. C., & Leuze, M. R. (1989). A theoretical investigation of a parallel genetic algorithm. In Schaffer, J. D. (Ed.), *Proceedings of the Third International Conference on Genetic Algorithms* (pp. 398–405). San Mateo, CA: Morgan Kaufmann.

Prabhu, D. (1996). *A study in massively parallel genetic algorithms with application to image interpretation.* Unpublished doctoral dissertation, Tulane University, New Orleans, LA.

Punch, W. F. (1998). How effective are multiple populations in genetic programming. In Koza, J. R., Banzhaf, W., Chellapilla, K., Deb, K., Dorigo, M., Fogel, D. B., Garzon, M. H., Goldberg, D. E., Iba, H., & Riolo, R. L. (Eds.), *Genetic Programming 98, Proceedings of the Third Annual Conference* (pp. 308–313). San Francisco: Morgan Kaufmann.

Punch, W. F., Averill, R. C., Goodman, E. D., Lin, S.-C., & Ding, Y. (1995). Design using genetic algorithms–Some results for laminated composite structures. *IEEE Expert, 10*(1), 42–49.

Punch, W. F., Goodman, E. D., Pei, M., Chia-Shun, L., Hovland, P., & Enbody, R. (1993). Further research on feature selection and classification using genetic algorithms. In Forrest, S. (Ed.), *Proceedings of the Fifth International Conference on Genetic Algorithms* (pp. 557–564). San Mateo, CA: Morgan Kaufmann.

Qi, X., & Palmieri, F. (1993). The diversification role of crossover in the genetic algorithms. In Forrest, S. (Ed.), *Proceedings of the Fifth International Conference on Genetic Algorithms* (pp. 132–137). San Mateo, CA: Morgan Kaufmann.

Reeves, C. R. (1993). Using genetic algorithms with small populations. In Forrest, S. (Ed.), *Proceedings of the Fifth International Conference on Genetic Algorithms* (pp. 92–99). San Mateo, CA: Morgan Kaufmann.

Robertson, G. G. (1987). Parallel implementation of genetic algorithms in a classifier system. In Grefenstette, J. J. (Ed.), *Proceedings of the Second International Conference on Genetic Algorithms* (pp. 140–147). Hillsdale, NJ: Lawrence Erlbaum Associates.

Rogers, A., & Prügel-Bennett, A. (1999). Modelling the dynamics of a steady state genetic algorithm. In Banzhaf, W., & Reeves, C. (Eds.), *Foundations of Genetic Algorithms 5* (pp. 57–68). San Francisco, CA: Morgan Kaufmann.

Rudolph, G. (1991). Global optimization by means of distributed evolution strategies. In Schwefel, H.-P., & Männer, R. (Eds.), *Parallel Problem Solving from Nature* (pp. 209–213). Berlin: Springer-Verlag.

Rudolph, G. (2000a). On takeover times in spatially structured populations: Array and ring. In Lai, K., Katai, O., Gen, M., & Lin, B. (Eds.), *Proceedings of the Second Asia-Pacific Conference on Genetic Algorithms and Applications* (pp. 144–151). Hong Kong: Global Link Publishing Company.

Rudolph, G. (2000b). Takeover times and probabilities of non-generational selection rules. In Whitley, D., Goldberg, D. E., Cantú-Paz, E., Spector, L., Parmee, I., & Beyer, H.-G. (Eds.), *GECCO-2000: Proceedings of the Genetic and Evolutionary Computation Conference* (pp. 903–910). San Francisco, CA: Morgan Kaufmann.

Sarma, J., & De Jong, K. (1996). An analysis of the effects of neighborhood size and shape on local selection algorithms. In Voigt, H.-M., Ebeling, W., Rechenberg, I., & Schwefel, H.-P. (Eds.), *Parallel Problem Solving from Nature, PPSN IV* (pp. 236–244). Berlin: Springer-Verlag.

Sarma, J., & De Jong, K. (1997). An analysis of local selection algorithms in a spatially structured evolutionary algorithm. In Bäck, T. (Ed.), *Proceedings of the Seventh International Conference on Genetic Algorithms* (pp. 181–187). San Francisco: Morgan Kaufmann.

Sarma, J., & De Jong, K. (1999). The behavior of spatially distributed evolutionary algorithms in non-stationary environments. In Banzhaf, W., Daida, J., Eiben, A. E., Garzon, M. H., Honavar, V., Jakiela, M., & Smith, R. E. (Eds.), *Proceedings of the Genetic and Evolutionary Computati on Conference* (pp. 572–578). San Francisco, CA: Morgan Kaufmann.

Schwefel, H. (1981). *Numerical optimization of computer models.* Chichester: John Wiley and Sons.

Schwehm, M. (1992). Implementation of genetic algorithms on various interconnection networks. In Valero, M., Onate, E., Jane, M., Larriba, J. L., & Suarez, B. (Eds.), *Parallel Computing and Transputer Applications* (pp. 195–203). Amsterdam: IOS Press.

Shapiro, B., & Navetta, J. (1994). A massively parallel genetic algorithm for RNA secondary structure prediction. *The Journal of Supercomputing, 8,* 195–207.

Sipper, M. (1997). *Evolution of parallel cellular machines: The cellular programming approach.* Heidelberg: Springer-Verlag.

Smith, J., & Vavak, F. (1999). Replacement strategies in steady state genetic algorithms: Static environments. In Banzhaf, W., & Reeves, C. (Eds.), *Foundations of Genetic Algorithms 5* (pp. 219–234). San Francisco, CA: Morgan Kaufmann.

Spiessens, P., & Manderick, B. (1991). A massively parallel genetic algorithm: Implementation and first analysis. In Belew, R. K., & Booker, L. B. (Eds.), *Proceedings of the Fourth International Conference on Genetic Algorithms* (pp. 279–286). San Mateo, CA: Morgan Kaufmann.

Sprave, J. (1994). Linear neighborhood evolution strategy. In Sebald, A. V., & Fogel, L. J. (Eds.), *Proceedings of the Third Annual Conference on Evolutionary Programming* (pp. 42–51). Singapore: World Scientific.

Sprave, J. (1999). A unified model of non-panmictic population structures in evolutionary algorithms. In Angeline, P. J., Michalewicz, Z., Schoenauer, M., Yao, X., & Zalzala, A. (Eds.), *Proceedings of the Congress on Evolutionary Computation,* Volume 2 (pp. 1384–1391). IEEE Press.

Stanley, T. J., & Mudge, T. (1995). A parallel genetic algorithm for multiobjective microprocessor design. In Eschelman, L. (Ed.), *Proceedings of the Sixth Interna-*

tional Conference on Genetic Algorithms (pp. 597–604). San Francisco, CA: Morgan Kaufmann.

Starkweather, T., Whitley, D., & Mathias, K. (1991). Optimization using distributed genetic algorithms. In Schwefel, H.-P., & Männer, R. (Eds.), *Parallel Problem Solving from Nature* (pp. 176–185). Berlin: Springer-Verlag.

Sterling, T. (1998). Beowulf-class clustered computing: Harnessing the power of parallelism in a pile of PCs. In Koza, J. R., Banzhaf, W., Chellapilla, K., Deb, K., Dorigo, M., Fogel, D. B., Garzon, M. H., Goldberg, D. E., Iba, H., & Riolo, R. L. (Eds.), *Genetic Programming 98* (pp. 883–887). San Francisco: Morgan Kaufmann.

Sumida, B. H., Houston, A. I., McNamara, J. M., & Hamilton, W. D. (1990). Genetic algorithms and evolution. *Journal of Theoretical Biology, 147*, 59–84.

Syswerda, G. (1989). Uniform crossover in genetic algorithms. In Schaffer, J. D. (Ed.), *Proceedings of the Third International Conference on Genetic Algorithms* (pp. 2–9). San Mateo, CA: Morgan Kaufmann.

Syswerda, G. (1991). A study of reproduction in generational and steady-state genetic algorithms. In Rawlins, G. J. E. (Ed.), *Foundations of Genetic Algorithms* (pp. 94–101). San Mateo, CA: Morgan Kaufmann.

Tamaki, H., & Nishikawa, Y. (1992). A paralleled genetic algorihtm based on a neighborhood model and its application to the jobshop scheduling. In Männer, R., & Manderick, B. (Eds.), *Parallel Problem Solving from Nature, 2* (pp. 573–582). Amsterdam: Elsevier Science.

Tanese, R. (1987). Parallel genetic algorithm for a hypercube. In Grefenstette, J. J. (Ed.), *Proceedings of the Second International Conference on Genetic Algorithms* (pp. 177–183). Hillsdale, NJ: Lawrence Erlbaum Associates.

Tanese, R. (1989a). Distributed genetic algorithms. In Schaffer, J. D. (Ed.), *Proceedings of the Third International Conference on Genetic Algorithms* (pp. 434–439). San Mateo, CA: Morgan Kaufmann.

Tanese, R. (1989b). *Distributed genetic algorithms for function optimization.* Unpublished doctoral dissertation, University of Michigan, Ann Arbor.

Thierens, D. (1995). *Analysis and design of genetic algorithms.* Doctoral dissertation, Katholieke Universiteit Leuven, Leuven, Belgium.

Thierens, D., & Goldberg, D. E. (1993). Mixing in genetic algorithms. In Forrest, S. (Ed.), *Proceedings of the Fifth International Conference on Genetic Algorithms* (pp. 38–45). San Mateo, CA: Morgan Kaufmann.

Thierens, D., & Goldberg, D. E. (1994). Convergence models of genetic algorithm selection schemes. In Davidor, Y., Schwefel, H.-P., & Männer, R. (Eds.), *Parallel Problem Solving fron Nature, PPSN III* (pp. 119–129). Berlin: Springer-Verlag.

Toffoli, T., & Margolus, N. (1987). *Cellular automata machines.* Cambriedge, MA: MIT Press.

Tomassini, M. (1993). The parallel genetic cellular automata: Application to global function optimization. In *Proceedings of the International Conference on Neural Networks and Genetic Algorithms* (pp. 385–391). Berlin: Springer-Verlag.

Tomassini, M. (1999). Parallel and distributed evolutionary algorithms: A review. In Miettinen, K., Mäkelä, M., Neittaanmäki, P., & Periaux, J. (Eds.), *Evolutionary Algorithms in Engineering and Computer Science* (pp. 113–133). Chichester, UK: J. Wiley and Sons.

Valenzuela-Rendón, M. (1989). *Two analysis tools to describe the operation of classifier systems.* Doctoral dissertation, University of Alabama, Tuscaloosa. Also available as TCGA Report No. 89005.

Whitley, D. (1989). The GENITOR algorithm and selective pressure: Why rank-Based allocation of reproductive trials is best. In Schaffer, J. D. (Ed.), *Proceedings of the Third International Conference on Genetic Algorithms* (pp. 116–121). San Mateo, CA: Morgan Kaufmann.

Whitley, D. (1993a). Cellular genetic algorithms. In Forrest, S. (Ed.), *Proceedings of the Fifth International Conference on Genetic Algorithms* (pp. 658). San Mateo, CA: Morgan Kaufmann.

Whitley, D. (1993b). An executable model of a simple genetic algorithm. In Whitley, L. D. (Ed.), *Foundations of Genetic Algorithms 2* (pp. 45–62). San Mateo, CA: Morgan Kaufmann.

Whitley, D., Rana, S., & Heckendorn, R. B. (1999). Exploiting separability in search: The island model genetic algorithm. *Journal of Computing and Information Technology*. forthcoming.

Whitley, D., & Starkweather, T. (1990). Genitor II: A distributed genetic algorithm. *Journal of Experimental and Theoretical Artificial Intelligence*, *2*, 189–214.

Wolpert, D., & Macready, W. (1997). No-free-lunch theorems for optimization. *IEEE Transactions on Evolutionary Computation*, *1*(1), 67–82.

Wright, S. (1932). The roles of mutation, inbreeding, crossbreeding and selection in evolution. In *Proceedings of the Sixth International Congress of Genetics* (pp. 356–366).

Zavanella, A., Giani, A., & Baiardi, F. (1998). On dropping niches in parallel genetic algorithms. In Koza, J. R., Banzhaf, W., Chellapilla, K., Deb, K., Dorigo, M., Fogel, D. B., Garzon, M. H., Goldberg, D. E., Iba, H., & Riolo, R. L. (Eds.), *Genetic Programming 98* (pp. 618). San Francisco: Morgan Kaufmann.

Zeigler, B. P., & Kim, J. (1993). Asynchronous genetic algorithms on parallel computers. In Forrest, S. (Ed.), *Proceedings of the Fifth International Conference on Genetic Algorithms* (pp. 660). San Mateo, CA: Morgan Kaufmann.

Index